Asahel N. Cole

The new Agriculture

Or, The Waters led Captive

Asahel N. Cole

The new Agriculture
Or, The Waters led Captive

ISBN/EAN: 9783337141332

Printed in Europe, USA, Canada, Australia, Japan

Cover: Foto ©ninafisch / pixelio.de

More available books at **www.hansebooks.com**

Your Friend,
A. N. Cole

THE NEW AGRICULTURE;

OR,

THE WATERS LED CAPTIVE.

BY

A. N. COLE.

ILLUSTRATED.

1885.
THE AMERICAN ANGLER,
NEW YORK.

DEDICATION.

This volume is respectfully dedicated to Dr. J. H. VINCENT, of Plainfield, New Jersey.

A. N. COLE.

HOME ON THE HILLSIDE, N. Y., October 1st, 1885.

PUBLISHERS' ANNOUNCEMENT.

In announcing the publication of this book the publishers would state that the claims of the author in behalf of his discoveries and methods seemed, when first presented to our attention, well nigh incredible. It was not until after a personal examination, at the "Home on the Hillside," of Mr. Cole's system of cultivation and an inspection of some of the wonderful resultant products, that we became thoroughly convinced that he has practically substantiated the claims set forth in this volume.

He could not have selected a more unpromising piece of land for testing the merits of "The New Agriculture." It was a steep and sterile hillside of Allegany hardpan, thinly covered with a soil, which was surface-washed and gullied by heavy rains and sun-baked in dry weather.

His system of culture based upon underground irrigation and fertilization maintained constantly and uniformly the year around by means of his own devising, after thirty years of investigation and study, has transferred this waste of ground, which nobody thought could be made profitably productive, into, comparatively speaking, a Garden of Eden. He simply makes "The New Agriculture" a willing Handmaid to Nature. He gathers and conserves in his trenches or subterranean reservoirs all the waters from dews, rains and melting snows, which, after equable filtration through the soil, are released at the foot of the slope in a never-failing stream of pure water at spring temperature. It would seem that not more than one-fifth of this fertilizing moisture is absorbed by a maximum crop. Fungus, that deadly foe to root growth, is completely eliminated. Drouth is forestalled and the ground in winter no more freezes than around a natural spring. The producing season in that latitude is elongated from forty to sixty days.

As to the expense of the new tillage, the improvement of the land in productiveness and the economies of the system in all ways, largely dispensing with the cost of plowing, spading and weeding and the use of expensive manures, turn every dollar of outlay into five at least in a short space of time. In a word, the roots of trees, shrubs and plants are constantly supplied, but never in surfeit, with the amount of moisture needed for their healthy and rapid growth and for the perfect development of leaf, bud, flower and fruit. These magnificent results are not, with us, matters of conjecture, nor have they been accepted without personal and careful inspection at Father Cole's "Home on the Hillside."

WM. C. HARRIS.
H. H. THOMPSON.

CONTENTS.

	Page.
THE LIFE OF A. N. COLE. BY HON. JOHN H. SELKREG	11–14
CHAPTER I.—THE DISCOVERY, DEVELOPMENT AND PUBLICATION OF THE NEW AGRICULTURE TO THE WORLD	15–81
CHAPTER II.—CIRCULATION OF WATER ON LAND—THE WONDERFUL MESILLA	82–99
CHAPTER III.—DESCRIPTION OF THE NEW SYSTEM—"HOME ON THE HILLSIDE"—THE HOT WATER SYSTEM	100–110
CHAPTER IV.—PRACTICAL RESULTS OF THE NEW SYSTEM	111–134
CHAPTER V.—THE INFLUENCE OF THE NEW AGRICULTURE UPON THE HEALTH OF MAN AND DOMESTIC ANIMALS—COMMUNICATION FROM THE HON. JOHN SWINBURNE—THE BANE OF FUNGUS BY PROFESSOR C. R. EARLEY	135–170
CHAPTER VI.—RECLAIMING THE GREAT AMERICAN DESERT	171–178
CHAPTER VII.—THE EXPENSE OF THE NEW SYSTEM	179–186
CHAPTER VIII.—1850—1885 "THE HOME ON THE HILLSIDE" THEN AND NOW	189–206
CHAPTER IX.—MANURING UNDER THE NEW SYSTEM—THE AMERICAN POMOLOGICAL SOCIETY—A WELCOME FOR ALL AT THE "HOME ON THE HILLSIDE"	207–223

ILLUSTRATIONS.

	Page.
Portrait of the Author	Frontispiece.
Basswood Cottage	23
"The Home on the Hillside"	45
The Old Apple Tree	63
Single Plum, natural size	75
Group of Plums, natural size	85
Diagrams of the New System	103
The Strawberry Bouquet	125
Strawberry, natural size	139
Diagram of Infected Stables and Outhouses	155
Group of Peas	175
Single Tomato Plant	181
Trellis of Tomatoes	187
Single Tomato, natural size	193
Specimens of Apples, natural size, from Old Apple Tree	199
Quince, natural size	209

THE LIFE OF A. N. COLE.

The life of the author of this book has been an eventful one and into it has been crowded far more than can be found in that of ordinary public men. Knowing this and deeming a brief biographical sketch of Mr. Cole would be of interest to the general reader, the following has been prepared from memorandums procured from him and from others who have held intimate acquaintance with him during his life.

Asahel N. Cole was born on the 15th of October, 1821, in the town of Freedom, Cattaraugus County, N. Y., and is therefore 64 years of age at date of the appearance of this volume. His father, Daniel Cole, was a descendant from the family settling Cole's Hill, at Plymouth, Mass., and his mother, of maiden name Joanna Williams, was a lineal descendant of Roger Williams, of Rhode Island.

Enjoying a very retentive memory and possessed of an exceedingly active mind, it is not to be wondered at that Mr. Cole has made his mark in political and other circles, and was connected with large enterprises, which commenced by him were before completion appropriated by others who enjoy the fruits of growth planted by his hand.

When but four and a half years old the father and mother of the author died. Thus thrown upon his own resources, he early commenced the "battle of life," and even now when above three score he has all the energy of youth and the fire of mature manhood in his nature.

He was adopted by foster parents residing at Pike, at that time part of Allegany, now Wyoming County, N. Y. Up to the age of sixteen, when his foster father died, he had received the barest elements of a common school education. Starting out he sought employment as best he might in canvassing the state of Ohio for an agricultural and horticultural publication entitled the BUCKEYE PLOUGHBOY, published at Cleveland. His early study of odd numbers of this little monthly and Poor Richard's Almanac beyond doubt had much to do with the important discoveries set forth in this volume.

The year 1839 was spent in Michigan, our author having by this time gained, through his limited studies, sufficient knowledge to commence teaching school, which he continued to do until the year 1844, and then deciding to abandon his plans of becoming a minister of the Methodist Episcopal Church, for which he had prepared himself, he turned merchant and lumberman, working hard in the woods for a livelihood.

Divisions in the Methodist Church, growing out of the issues of slavery and anti-slavery, were the occasion of this new departure. Young Cole, interesting himself in politics, became an ardent Free Soiler, and, having patrons in the persons of Gerrit Smith and James S. Wadsworth, both large landowners in the timbered sections of Allegany County, his acquaintance and agreement with them politically brought, not only the gentlemen above named but many others, leaders of the free soil movement, to the side of a man from ten to twenty years younger than themselves. When the revolutionary period of 1848 was reached, and A. N. Cole was but twenty-seven years of age, he was better known by, and more closely linked with, Joshua R. Giddings, Gerrit Smith, James S. Wadsworth, William H. Seward, Charles Sumner, Salmon P. Chase, John P. Hale, John Van Buren and others of like political affinities, than any man of his age in America.

What made him especially a most important factor in the politics of the period was his close attachment to and alliance with Horace Greeley, whose acquaintance he formed so early as 1843. Mr. Cole became the trusted personal, private and confidential correspondent of this great journalist, and thus remained to the close of Mr. Greeley's life in 1872.

In the meantime Mr. Cole had, so early as 1852, assisted by General James S. Wadsworth, established the GENESEE VALLEY FREE PRESS as a Republican paper at his home in Allegany County. In the columns of this, the pioneer Republican newspaper of the country, appeared the first call for a convention to organize the Republican party. This convention met at Friendship, N. Y., in May, 1854, and dates the birth of the Republican party, though the town of Angelica, N. Y., succeeded in 1884 in establishing her birthright by showing that the first convention called for nominating candidates convened at that place about the middle of October, 1854. The celebration of the birth of the party took place at Angelica just before last fall's (1884) election. A. N. Cole presided, having been for years acknowledged and recognized as the Father of the Republican Party.

It is not however, in politics or public life where Mr. Cole has won his proudest laurels. He never held but one important public trust, that of readjuster or reassessor of income taxes in the Second district of Brooklyn for a period of about one year of the first term of President Grant, receiving his appointment from Secretary Boutwell. Mr. Cole held court in revenue cases with such energy, force and knowledge of the revenue laws as to gain his admittance to practice in all the courts of the state, receiving his diploma at a general term of court held at Poughkeepsie in May, 1868. Before this, however, he had been waited upon by the solid New York delegation of Republican Senators and Members of Congress from the State of New York for appointment to the office of Internal Revenue Supervisor for the Metropolitan District, but President Johnson interposing objections the Hon. Silas B. Dutcher received the appointment.

Up to this period Mr. Cole had only been known as a journalist of wide influence, but he had also won laurels without number at Albany for his advocacy of measures for improvement of the cities of New York and Brooklyn, and as early as 1877 saw carried through the experiment in Greenwich Street testing the question of practicability of the elevated railroad system as now in operation in the metropolis. General John A. Dix and the Hon. S. L. M. Barlow, associated with others, employed Mr. Cole as advocate and attorney, breaking the powerful combinations of opposing interests to the system of rapid transit now existing.

The energy and earnestness of Mr. Cole up to this period had produced a marked impression on the public, and he was recognized as the trusted and confidential friend of the highest officials in national and state governments. He was selected to have charge of the bill reorganizing the Erie Railway, which when perfected and passed saved that great work from wreck and ruin.

Governor Cornell in 1880 signed the bill granting to a company to be organized, the abandoned Genesee Valley Canal for railroad purposes. This achievement came of seven years of persistent labor on the part of Mr. Cole, saving to the population of the Genesee Valley a magnificent property otherwise lost. The syndicate finally securing the grant, mortgaged it for two millions of dollars, while the solitary individual (A. N. Cole) who practically did the work secured a merest fraction of the amount for labor and expense in securing the grant. Twice in his life the author of the New Agriculture, worked down and out, has succumbed for a few months at a time, and his work has seemed at an end, the tax upon his energies being such as to apparently break him down.

About four years ago his neighbors were astonished by the growth of fruits and vegetables of marvelous size, beauty, profusion and perfection upon his grounds. He was understood at first as making experiments in under drainage, nor did his nearest neighbors and most intimate friends have an intelligent conception of the methods under which he was proceeding—those of subsurface, subterranean or underground irrigation, better known as "The New Agriculture."

And so it is that, to a man who never had to exceed three years of education at school, has been left the discovery of the fundamental laws governing the movements of the waters upon and beneath the soil, which the writer of this brief biography, the publishers of this volume and many others who have visited "The Home on the Hillside" unite in believing will effect a revolution in the present systems of agriculture. J. H. SELKREG.

ITHACA, N. Y., October 15, 1885.

CHAPTER I.

THE DISCOVERY, DEVELOPMENT AND PUBLICATION OF "THE NEW AGRICULTURE" TO THE WORLD.

That there is a divinity shaping the ends of mortals, the author of this volume deems a certainty. In no other way is it possible to account for the inevitable. Solomon had it right when he said: "There is a time for all things under the sun." The time would seem to have come when the waters may be so controlled, as to pass them through soils, rather than allow them, as hitherto, to find their way from summits to plains and valleys along their surfaces. What has been done by the individual in this respect, is to be done ere long by the multitude. The immensity of such an undertaking, is calculated to discourage, at first, the bravest and most hopeful. The Chinese wall, the pyramids and other evidences, all along the track of time, indicate that great undertakings have only to be persevered in, and the end is ultimately reached.

Were every farmer or land-holder having lands situated on hillsides, slopes and inclines, to put but a single acre in condition to gather in, house, husband, handle and control the waters falling down during the year, such would be the scene of transformation, as to make an end of hesitation and doubt. Could a model acre be shown in each county of every state and territory of our Union, a decade would not pass before spades would everywhere be found to be trumps, and such would be the multiplication of means for holding and handling the waters, as to result within a single generation, to an approach to transformation of the earth's surface.

Upon the author of this volume has devolved the work of making a beginning. As things look at this time of writing it seems probable, that by the tenth of July, 1885, two acres of a model five under treatment, will be in condition to show what can be done to control and use the waters for purposes of agriculture and horticulture. Not under three years, however, will our model five acres be so perfected, as to make a complete demonstration of anything like the utmost possibilities. How it has all occurred that the author has been the one to find out the way, and seeking and finding, to lead the van of this, one of the greatest of works yet devolved upon man, will be understood as the story is told of a lifetime spent in following the waters. I was eight years of age when I read in "Poor Richard's Almanac" that :

"If the farmer or gardener would know the difference in fruitage, between a tree left to turf about its roots, and one where the soil is loosened, let him try the experiment."

In our garden were plum trees bearing, to a most gratifying degree. These were on rich soil, with wash from the barnyard. Bait for trout-fishing was here obtained ; the angle or earth-worm, in abundance. To loosen the soil about the roots of these trees, became correspondingly a pastime and profit. That the plums would grow larger, and their flavor be improved, Dr. Franklin had said, and of course he knew. Suffice it to say that the loosening seemed to call for a pushing away at the trunks, till their roots took only weak hold in the ground. It was, if we recollect, in the spring of 1829, when we were scarcely nine years of age, that the trees thus treated, refused to put out bud or blossom, nor so much as gave evidence of life. From that hour, losing faith in Poor Richard's Almanac, we followed thereafter our own inclination and methods. How many were the plants taken up and put back into their own or new places we cannot now say. To examine their roots, and find out their ways of germination, became a passion. Nothing so disturbed us as the wrong end up in which the beans came out of the ground. Why again should the potatoes grow beneath the soil, and the balls upon the tops of the vines, was a puzzle to us. Peas the fourth of July, and cucumbers the middle of that month, with which to give keener relish for our trout, was an ever yearning ambition.

We think it was at about the age of twelve, when we came across a newspaper mention of an experiment which we decided to forthwith make. This was one with which nearly everybody has become familiar; that of a tight barrel set on end, and filled with round stones so far up as the open bung, then shingled with flat stones, and these covered with straw and a coating of coarse manure, finishing up by filling the barrel with rich earth, and planting on this a hill of cucumbers. The handiest barrel was accordingly seized upon, that used by our foster mother for pounding clothes. We began operations in earnest, but conflict ensued, since it was impossible to convince our maternal guide that her pounding barrel was the spot in which to grow pickles. Threats of castigation did not deter us from persistence, and promising our mother another and better barrel within a few days, we went defiantly ahead with our "gardening." The maternal word was kept to the letter, but this was something of daily discipline, and so we did not seriously object to it, in view of the harvest in prospect.

Our experiment was made with care, since we had found out thus early, that what was worth doing at all, was worth well doing. Our one hill of cucumbers did wonders, and yet came far short of a barrel of pickles. We estimated them at a half bushel, but now, having gotten over the ardor of youth, we are bound to admit that they would have filled only a peck measure, and possibly have come short of that by at least "one pickle." But the pounding barrel having been ruined, and the "rod in pickle" having been applied, and the crop falling far short of our expectations, we resolved not to give it up so, but repeated our experiment the ensuing year, well convinced that we could demonstrate the fact that a pounding barrel was a good place in which to grow pickles ; and the second time we succeeded in an eminent degree, since the one hill, in the barrel, produced nearly or quite a half bushel, and doing the picking ourselves, and the barrel being in close proximity to a fine patch in the garden, we convinced our foster mother that her boy was a prodigy in growing cucumbers ; nor told a lie any more than would George Washington probably have done under similar circumstances, but left our mother to tell the story of her boy having grown a full half barrel of pickles from one hill, planted in her pounding barrel.

In the season of 1840, finding ourself in Michigan, we made careful note of the good effects upon grasses and grains in proximity to the primeval forests, more especially in fields lying below the level of the wilderness in which the maple, beech, basswood and other like timbers prevailed ; nor did the corresponding dearth in fields on and about the prairies and oak-openings, escape observation. Again, in tracing what we presumed were tracks of hidden waters beneath the surface operating as we conjectured as inlets and outlets, connecting multitudinous lakes, ponds, swamps and morasses, covered in many instances with turf trembling upon their surfaces, we remarked the deep green of the verdure, when contrasted with that of grasses and grains on more elevated planes, and along undulations.

From Lower California, far away on the Pacific coast, rumors came of a valley of green amid the sands of the desert, perennial in products of the olive and vine, where buried were the waters of a river in subterranean flow, and where the roots of trees and plants, deep dipping down, found nourishment at a depth of from twenty to thirty feet. In reading of the Sahara and other deserts of earth, the oasis was our only solace, and how to grow an oasis, became a study of intensest interest. The artesian well we longed to look upon, nor could we be satisfied till our eyes had seen it.

Returning to our native state of New York in the autumn of that year, the green of the grasses of Allegany and Wyoming Counties, as seen amid the sere and yellow leaf, begat dreams of a land somewhere hidden from view, in which no deserts are found, and where grasses greenly growing, alongside of flowers unfading, and fruits that perish not as apples of the Dead Sea, turning to ashes in the hands of men, but growing ever on amid immortelles of the great hereafter, made the gloomy winter of 1839 and '40, to appear the less dark and dreary, on account of our dreamings.

The next Spring, Summer and Autumn were spent in looking over, from time to time, that delightful section of Western New York, embraced in the valleys of the Genesee River and its numberless tributaries, noting, more especially, those outgushing fountains of living waters, appearing as springs, chiefest among which are those at Caledonia, Avon and Wethersfield. The Oatka, Honeoye, Tonawanda, Canaseraga, Cohocton, Canisteo and other creeks and rivers, come largely from springs bubbling out all along their channel ways. Tracing these waters to their sources, and dwelling upon the methods employed by the Creator in begetting springs, rivers, rivulets and lakes, we learned lessons of incalculable value. On return therefore from Michigan to Wyoming County, New York, we drifted as naturally back to the Cattaraugus of our birth, and Allegany of our breeding, as follows the trout in ascent to the sources of streams amid the forests and among the mountains.

From early childhood, we had had liquid manures on the brain. So early as 1844, we undertook to grow a few cabbages to impressive proportions, for the sole purpose of convincing the champion cabbage grower of our acquaintance that there were things in heaven and earth not so much as dreamed of in his conceited philosphy. We had barely set out in life, and occupying a rented house, had the narrowest limits for garden making. A few rows of potatoes, a bed of beets, another of onions, lettuce, etc., to which was added a few cabbage plants, made up the sum of our venture. Near by dwelt the boss farmer and gardener of the neighborhood, Squire C. Our ground was rich, and we could not understand why the Squire had fine cabbage, while ours had scarcely begun heading.

"What do you do, Squire," we asked, "to make your cabbage grow so rapidly?"

With a mischievous twinkle of the eye, our venerable neighbor answered:

"That's a secret worth knowing, and if you will not tell anybody, and try it yourself, I'll let you know how it's done."

We promised, of course; when coming up closely, the old gentleman whispered in our ear:

"I always hoe my cabbage before sunrise."

Forthwith we resolved to get even with him. Our plants were fine ones, thrifty growing, and we had somewhere heard that weak brine turned upon the soil was a good thing for cabbage, and having heard also that hen manure was best of all fertilizers, our mind was made up instanter, to show our neighbor the Squire, what could be done in growing cabbages in absence of early rising. Providing ourself therefore with a solution of salt, hen manure, and adding ashes and lime as ingredients, we set about rebuking our neighbor for even hinting that we were the identical individual pointed out in Proverbs, 6th chapter, 6th verse, etc.

Rising early each morning for a week, we "doctored" our cabbages, in confident belief that, in the course of a month or six weeks, we would be able to show neighbor Couch what a boy knew about growing cabbage. It took just six days to *kill every plant* as dead as so many Egyptian mummies. From that hour, though sticking to theories of liquid manuring, we gave up that sort of "doctoring" which applies it in allopathic doses.

On page 65 of Mr. Stewart's book on irrigation for the farm, garden and orchard may be found the following:

"In applying liquid manure it is always necessary to use it in a highly diluted state, even so much diluted that if it would run off perfectly clear it might be found of sufficient strength for all purposes. The danger lies in using it of too great strength, rather than in diluting it too copiously."

We did not mention to our venerable Mentor, the Squire, the results arising from our use of liquid manuring, but we ceaselessly sought the rule to follow in compounding them and what proportions of potassium, ammonia, lime, sodium, magnesia and other elements of liquids and solids are required, for this and that crop, in order to obtain the best results.

Not far from five years subsequent to our experiment in growing cabbage, we found ourself occupying a home on the banks of the

Genesee. In our farm barn yard manures had lain for years in huge piles, from the bases of which ran off streams of liquid, dark as lye, distributing and diffusing their influence over three or four acres of alluvial lying between the barn and the river. In the track of this current of inspiration to plant growth, stood a pine stump with a breadth of top telling the story of one of those departed giants of the forest, occasionally found in the wilderness of this region at the commencement of the present century. That some pioneer had attempted, years before, to grub out this stump, and after making a good beginning, abandoned the undertaking, was evidenced by the fact that on its upper side toward the barn, was an excavation telling the tale of the undertaker. Into this hole the liquids from the barn had been discharging for years, and sinking below the surface their subterranean track was plainly marked by a wealth of verdure the equal to which we had never before seen. Immediately below the stump grew a most wonderful blackberry bush, the canes at base averaging an inch in diameter, and growing to a length of from twelve to fifteen feet. From this one bush, our family picked nearly a bushel of native blackberries, rivaling in beauty, and greatly superior in flavor to any we had ever tasted.

Here was evidence conclusive that to Mother Earth may at all times safely be left the work of elaboration, combination, compounding, mixing and mingling of ingredients necessary to the germination, growth and development of plants.

In Beers' Illustrated history of Allegany County, page 362, may be found a picture of Basswood cottage, the home in the wilderness where we made in reality, our first garden ; hence, what would perhaps otherwise seem inappropiate, becomes fit and opportune, and we make a quotation from the history, as follows :

"Basswood Cottage, the home to which Mr. Cole and family had

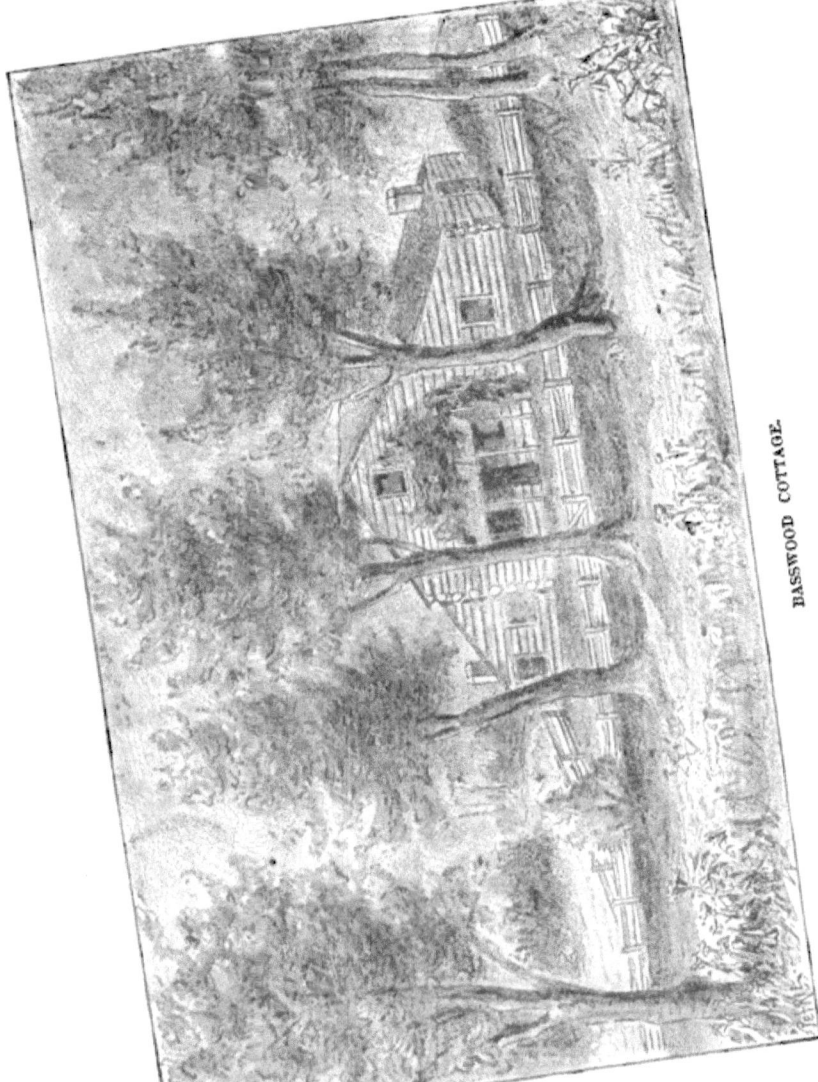

BASSWOOD COTTAGE.

retreated, represented in accompanying engraving, was a log cabin in the pine woods, and is thus pictured by the graphic pen of the since widely known journalist, in one of his easy chair letters, appearing in the Elmira *Advertiser*, under date of February 24th, 1875."

"The spot chosen for our dwelling place was as wild, sylvan and rustic as any to be found amid the forests primeval of Allegany Co., N. Y. Our house was one built of logs, unhewn, but not rudely so, or without architectural pretentions in an humble way—a neat cottage with wings, portico in front, over which ran climbing roses, while ivies twined, and morning glories in sinuous wanderings and windings found their way to the roof of the cottage. Flowers bloomed in the dooryard, planted, cared for and watered by the ever busy hand of 'Mrs. Easy Chair.' In the rear of the house was a lofty hill quite like to a mountain, from the base to the brow of which rose up tall pines, oaks, maples, beeches, birches and basswoods, whose shadows fell upon us daily, as the sun went down before its time in the west. In the front and to the north was a carpet of greensward, partially shaded by beautiful trees, planted by nature's plastic hand, and scattered here and there were maples of second growth with spreading branches. On the left was a garden, where was early cultivated that taste for horticulture since grown to be a passion."

Yes, dear reader, it was here, amid the shadows of the forest, we made our first garden. The spot was a pocket of alluvial, rich, deep and dark, less than an half acre, created by drift from the mountain side above, pure vegetable mold; no spot could have well been richer in soil, or more naturally productive. Here were grown such potatoes, peas, beans, cabbages, turnips and other garden vegetables, as we have never seen until the adoption of our present system of culture.

Few stone were found in the soil. Here and there, however, buried and out of sight, was found an occasional pine or hemlock knot, resisting for generations the tooth of time. Here we found the first clump-foot cabbage, and forthwith, suspecting something was not quite right, we dug down, and brought out a huge pine knot. . Here, again, we began experiments with Hovey's seedling, succeeding after a year or two of patient endeavor, in gathering from a bed of thirty hills nearly a pint of strawberries, the largest specimen of which measured three inches in circumference. So great was our triumph that one of our friends traveled on foot six miles to see that big berry. Were our friend now near by, instead of far away we would, were he to visit us next July, 1885, show him bushels of berries, averaging as large as the one, which at that time, was the greatest of wonders. When it comes to specimens of our best, viz : Jersey Queens, Jumbos, Manchesters, Monarchs, &c., we could exhibit them by scores and hundreds, measuring from five to seven inches in circumference.

But the reason of the barrenness of most of our strawberry plants in our first garden puzzled and vexed us to find out, as it probably did every other producer in our county. While onions grew to larger size than we had seen anywhere, and cabbages, beets and turnips astonished us with their prodigious growth, only about one out of three of our strawberry plants showed berries. The vines appeared sickly, and the roots of the plants did not seem to get firm hold in the earth, and we took to pulling them up, and digging down, seeking the cause of infecundity and unthrift. With scarce an exception, we found at the depth of from twelve to fifteen inches the inevitable pine or hemlock knot, and still more frequently, a flat stone. We found the roots of our plants, reaching deeply down, had come in contact with buried obstructions, and that disease had followed. Making use of the spectacles of an aged person serving admirably as a microscope, and securing a focus best calculated to bring out the hidden enemy, it did not take long for us to become satisfied that the seed of fungus was nearly everywhere present, the great begetter of disease. Of this seed of fungus we had read much in books, found in the library of a physician, in whose family we spent much time in early life.

Suffice it to say that we were thirty years old before we became convinced of the baleful influence of this arch enemy of plant growth. We found it amid damps and moulds, and equally amid soils in which was a lack of moisture. Wherever the roots of plants came in contact with sticks covered with mould, or with stones hidden in the soil, more especially with the inevitable flat stone completely destructive of plant thrift, we found fungus, bringing decay and death. Nor was this all, for hovering about the roots of plants diseased from infection by fungus, were found parasites in form of the wire-worm, earth-worm and more especially the minute white grub or maggot, the latter fatally destructive, eating away the roots of plants, and bringing not merely disease, but certain death.

In a few instances, so deep down did we dip to find the offender, as to reach the subsoil, evenly and smoothly descending to the stream flowing alongside our little delta, so rich in surface as to enable us to grow more on our single half acre than was gathered from two to three times the area devoted to gardening by neighboring farmers.

During our first year's experience, there came sudden showers of such force and volume, as to bring from off the mountain side above, an amount of soil and debris from the recesses of the forest as to convince us that a ditch, sunk at the base of the hill and connecting with the stream traversing the valley, would be just the thing to provide against accidents. Plowing our garden late in autumn, we took the precaution to direct the plowman to leave a deep furrow as near the base of the hill as convenient. This was done, and here was found what had seemingly been a channel for waters, or from conformation of the ground, more probably such a receptacle as to send them in even flow along the subsoil to the stream, leaving the mold in their track, and begetting our little pocket of a garden. Applying the pick and spade, our ditch was completed, but as this in its curve described a crescent, with point terminating in the bed of the creek up the stream, discharge of the waters into the creek only took place when the 'dish' overflowed. To prevent our trench from filling with soil therefore, recourse was had to filling it with stone, a quantity of which had been thrown out by the plow, and so a burial spot was made for stone and knots, old boots, shoes and other castaways of the household, in promiscuous minglings. Over these was cast the pure vegetable mold, and thus, in descending the hillside, the waters dropped into the trench, and thence flowed along the dip of the subsoil, until in subterranean movement they reached the stream. In the sinking of our ditch, not so much as a dream had we, that demonstration was being made of a method which was to ultimate in so modifying antecedent systems of farming and gardening, as to amount to what now looks like revolution. And yet so it proved in more ways than one, since it was this crudely conceived and carelessly sunken trench, with its surface of sponge, that told a story to be yet heard all over the world.

Not least of good fortunes was the one of emergence, at base of our mountain side, of considerable numbers of minute springs, even in the driest of weather, whose waters in spring, autumn and winter, warmly descending from what may be fitly denominated "our great dipper" on the mountain side above, supplied the household with excellent water. Finding the waters lost in the depths of our ditch, we ascended the slope and arrested them by making a second ditch, thus aggregating the waters at the rear of the house, and, the winter proving an open one, we secured a fountain of pure water during its continuance. The snows in the woods began melting in February, and their waters descending the hill, striking the surface of our trench, disappeared, only to emerge in the stream beyond, and all along through the spring ensuing seemed to render more crystal-clear the waters of the creek. The effect upon the soil of our garden seemed miraculous; for such was its condition as to enable us to plant potatoes the last days of February, doing so in hopes of being able to mature them in season to avoid the rot, at that time threatening extinction of this most valuable among root crops.

Not until within the last ten years have we been enabled to see that it was the waters of rains, dews and spring melting snows, descending from among the damps and moulds, mosses, ferns, flags, wild grasses, mucks and minglings of a swamp in the depression of that mountain side above, moving out from under the snows at spring water temperature and dropping into our trench and continuing to flow along the incline of the subsoil—not for ten years did we discover that these waters removed the frost from our garden, preparing it for germination of seeds two or three weeks earlier than otherwise.

We see it all now, having found out there was the best of reasons existing why we, that season, grew as fine potatoes as we had ever seen, the frost having been kept out of the ground during March when the Frost King coming in fiercest fury, laid his hand on the lands of our neighbors, freezing them to a considerable depth, fully three weeks after we had committed our seed to the ground, and making an end of crops on every other spot, within, perhaps, an hundred miles in any direction from our home. Nor was it alone the condition of the soil as regarded temperature, but so even and uniform was the flow of the waters, and so perfectly were food and drink supplied to the tubers, food always in abundance and never in surfeit, that the effects of fungus, about that period developing infection of soils on both sides of the Atlantic, and that very season reducing the potato crop to a point threatening extinction, did not touch our little patch of about a quarter of an acre, and we harvested fully thirty bushels of potatoes in beauty of perfection. This was so much a matter of surprise to our neighbors, that the ensuing spring they took to early planting as a remedy for the blight; but nobody seemed to realize benefits from so doing, since the season succeeding proved equally one of blight and destruction, so far as the potato was concerned.

That season, the last spent in Basswood Cottage, was the one at date of which practically began the work of our discoveries.

Though meeting Horace Greeley from time to time, from 1843 to 1861, counseling with and confiding in him as in none other among public men of our country, it was not until the latter year that our relations became those of intimate companionship. Though honoring and esteeming Salmon P. Chase, Charles Sumner, William H. Seward, Joshua R. Giddings, Gerrit Smith, James S. Wadsworth, Abraham Lincoln and hundreds of others we might name, advising with and confiding in them, Mr. Greeley was the only one we had never found at fault on questions affecting the health and wealth of earth's peoples. This deep thinking and profound moral and political philosopher, a second Doctor Franklin, has had no equal in our judgement among the public men of our country.

John C. Fremont, the Pathfinder, had but little more than made search for those passes over and through which, first the weary wagon train, and since then long successions of steam cars have coursed their iron way, linking ocean with ocean, when Horace

Greeley by stage, on horseback and on foot, made his overland journey to California. At the time of setting out the editor of the *Tribune* had a better knowledge of the composition of soils and their adaptation to the growth of this and that crop, than perhaps any man of his day and generation. Profoundly believing the way would be ultimately found to make the desert to blossom as the rose, Mr. Greeley, before starting on his journey, during a most interesting conversation on the subject of reclaiming desert lands, said to us that he would not think of going were it not for an irrepressible desire to see and determine for himself whether there existed, in fact, an American desert. On his return, meeting our friend and Mentor at Hornellsville by appointment, he said:

"I want to see and talk with you, Cole, and tell you all about what I have seen. Let me say to you now that Clark, Lewis and Fremont were greater discoverers than Christopher Columbus. Columbus found a new world, albeit his discovery was made at a time when navigators of a half dozen nations were finding their way into distant and unexplored seas and oceans, and he only followed in the track of predecessors, though more adventurous as he was braver and more intelligent and intuitive, than others of his day and generation. But, my dear fellow, this new world that Columbus discovered is about being rediscovered; and these Horatios all about us, are to find out there are millions of things in heaven and earth they have never dreamed of in their philosophies. The South is a great country, cursed with madmen, fancying themselves statesmen and sages, men who cannot be convinced that the fetters forged for their slaves, and the chains about the bodies of their bondsmen are not those of iron, but of flax and tow, which, at the touch of fire are bound first or last to turn to ashes all, and the places knowing now the oppressed and oppressor to know them no more forever.

"I have made a long journey, and seen more, and learned more than in all my life before. Ours is the greatest country, and this is the greatest people on the face of the earth. England, France, Germany and all the other nations of Europe are as old men, their energies exhausted, their resources largely wasted, and their possibilities thoroughly tested. There is more of gold and silver and of precious stones in our great American desert, than in all of the countries of the Old World, and among the hills, along the plains, and in the valleys of the Rocky Mountain and Sierra Nevada and Coast Ranges, and along the Pacific slope, are found greater possibilities as regards population and production than in all of the older sections of our own country, or, in fact, any other portion of our globe. I want to tell you about those big trees, and all of the other big and little things I have seen since I have been gone. I will only say now that Sumner had it right. We ought to buy the slaves of their masters and pay for them, if to do this, as Sumner says, it becomes necessary to build a bridge of gold over which these bondsmen may cross in reaching a land of liberty. We can afford to build it. There is money enough in the mines of California now being dug out to buy the whole South, lands, cotton, corn, slaves and slaveholders, and colonize them all in Africa together, or somewhere else, if need be. But colonization is a fraud, a delusion and a snare. There is work enough, and will be found wages enough, for all sorts of workers inside the boundaries of what has been denominated the great American desert, to employ an hundred millions of white and black men alike. It's all a lie, that because people are black they will not work. Who built the pyramids? Who the Chinese wall? Who was Hannibal?

"The Egyptians were no more a white people four thousand years ago than now. I tell you the Carthagenians had no more physical and intellectual power three thousand years ago than have the Nubians and Abyssinians of to-day. This whole thing of black and white, and all this nonsense about white men taking more to work than black ones, is only an excuse for enslavement. Let me tell you that white people do very little work south. John M. Botts understands it, as also does Cassius M. Clay. Everybody who knows enough to keep out of the fire, North and South alike, understands it, but people are not generally honest enough to confess it.

"I have been out among all sorts of folks who work, and if I except the Indians, people of any and all nations will work, only give them freedom, free soil, and an opportunity to secure free homes. Possibly the Indians will work also, should any be left at the close of the present century, which I very much doubt, since whiskey and the vices of mean white men are rapidly making an end of our aboriginal tribes, and I think sometimes that the sooner the thing is done and the last Indian's grave is dug the better. I believe in God and his providence; you know I do, Cole, but what is providence so far as Indians go, God only knows. Come down to the city and see me, dear Cole, and give me a chance to tell you about my over land journey."

Such was the tenor of what Mr. Greeley said at Hornellsville. A month later found us in New York for three or four days, a considerable portion of the time being spent in the company of America's greatest journalist. How to reclaim the desert by irrigation, was the burden of Mr. Greeley's every discourse. Artesian wells, windmills, current-wheels and other methods of lifting the waters from levels below to inclines and planes above, was a subject he continually dwelt upon. Mr. Stewart, in his admirable book on page 23 says:

"The late Horace Greeley, who, although an enthusiast on the subject of irrigation, was nearly correct in his estimate, when he concluded that one artesian well would serve to irrigate no more than a quarter section of land, or one hundred and sixty acres."

When discoursing on artesian wells, we asked Mr. Greeley if he felt confident that water would be reached in a majority of instances, if the experiment of sinking such wells was made in the arid portions of our country. His answer, given in the affirmative, was coupled with hesitation, and he concluded by saying, that while he was quite confident, he was so doubtful at times about it, as to experience a feeling of despondency, since the resources of the richest portion of our country could only be developed by ample water supplies.

With his usual clearness of vision, he made frequent mention of a faith within him, that the time would come when those seas and oceans of water, descending in rivers of ceaseless flow from the melting of snows and ices upon the summits of great ranges, would in some way be arrested, held back and made use of for purposes of irrigation. Solar evaporation, as he impressively declared, was the great obstacle to success in this direction.

"Dam up these waters as you may," he said, "and hold them back as you will, or move them forward, that tongue of fire which comes from a sky completely cloudless from April to November, with the mercury ranging from eighty to one hundred and fifty degrees between sunrise and sunset of each day, leaves little hope for such a system of water preserve and supply as will gather them in for mechanical, manufacturing and mining purposes, to say nothing of domestic uses or those of irrigation."

In one of these conversations, Mr. Greeley made mention of the reported existence in Southern California, if our memory serves us well, in the neighborhood of Los Angeles, where, in the midst of a desert, was seen an oasis so remarkable as to occasion surprise. This was a valley, as described to him, of perpetual green, along which for several miles was found growing at all seasons of the year, such fruits, flowers and profuse vegetation as scarcely anywhere else seen on the face of the earth. Dipping down, at the depth of twenty-two feet, there was found a sunken river three or four feet deep, and a mile or two broad. This concealed river, one of crystal waters, was what begat the oasis. To see for himself, Mr. Greeley assured us, so became a passion, and that there were days together, when he felt he could not return home without looking in upon this wonderful valley. He returned, bringing with him the evidence of those he deemed credible witnesses and having in his mind no doubt about its existence, and furthermore that all along this wonderful subterranean river the roots of trees, and even of the wild clover and other productions of Southern California, reached the waters in their dippings down.

These conversations with our most trusted counsellor and friend, had great influence, and the subject of subsurface, subterranean or underground flow of the waters as a means of irrigation, became more and more a constant study. That a deep covering of earth would shield the waters from solar evaporation was evident. The law of gravity inclining the waters to sink into the earth, and another law, that of capillary attraction, quite as mysterious, magical, powerful and all-pervading, became at once a source of constant study and observation.

While according to Mr. Greeley the credit and honor of being a continual prompter, intensifying our lines of thought, not to him, however, or to any other one man, but to individuals, here and there met with, in a majority of instances, comparatively speaking, unlearned, or rather, unlettered men, we gained most of knowledge. It was during our residence in Brooklyn that from an ex-slave black as Othello, at blackest painted, we learned how lands were reclaimed in the neighborhood of the Dismal Swamp. From the Hollander we found out how dykes were constructed, and from an unlettered son of the Emerald Isle we learned how fuel was secured in the bogs of his native Ireland. It was from the Germans, however, that we obtained most valuable information. Intelligent, as a rule, patient workers, staid, steady, sober thinkers, slow-going, and yet sure, we found them always good authority on matters of soil and production, irrigation and drainage.

Reading the *Tribune* daily, we never omitted to note what our friend Greeley and his former editorial associates had to say about farming and gardening. Forming the acquaintance and becoming warmly attached to Col. D. D. T. Moore, of the old *Rural New Yorker*, and getting acquainted with Mr. Andrew S. Fuller, a companionable and remarkably well-informed gentleman connected with the *Tribune*, we asked them and nearly everybody else with whom we conversed, what each thought about the waste of the waters coming of ordinary methods of tiling and drainage with stone drains.

Though not saying a word about it to anyone, we could not help feeling provoked at seeing mankind indulging in what seemed to us a wicked folly, amounting to madness, as they made haste to get the waters out into seas and oceans, instead of using them while on the lands, and only conducting portions of the surplus down to the sea levels.

From 1866 to 1870 we were formulating plans and devising methods of drainage, which should at once irrigate lands and provide against stagnation of the waters, and coming across the stray writings of Major Hugh T. Brooks, of Wyoming County, N. Y., he seemed to us the man who had found out things which all of the world ought to know by intuition. But having heard people say that "what Horace Greeley and Hugh T. Brooks didn't know about farming" would fill a much larger book than what a regiment of that sort of farmers did know, we felt doubtful as regarded our own views, not being any sort of a farmer at all, and concluded that what Major Brooks and ourself had found out about drainage would do to keep. We bided our time, for it occurred to us that it might do those of our neighbors good, who had been poking sticks and making game of our "mining for myths," should they care to learn how to do it, rather than hold on to their ways of how not to do it; that to secure a patent and insist on their paying moderately for right of "mining" would increase their graces, and so we kept our own counsel.

The old year of 1884 was waning, and the new one 1885 about being ushered in, when we came across the following from the pen of Col. Curtis:

"Farmers in 1882 expended $5,500,000 for tile and dug nearly 53,000 miles of drains to put them in. Besides, thousands of miles were laid with stones. Tile-makers and theorists have created and fostered this craze, and if continued it will result in a perpetual water famine. Wholesale rules adopted without discrimination are a big curse in agriculture, and drainage is one of the most potent for mischief. It is true that in many cases drainage improves land and makes it more tillable, but not always more fertile. Oftentimes a wet lot, or a wet patch, will, on account of the wetness produce more grass than any other portion of the farm, and by being let alone supplies some spring which is invaluable. The drain fever seizing the owner, the water is speedily carried off, the early and constant pasture spoiled, and the spring fed from it destroyed. Does this outlay pay? The same thoughtless improvement sends the melting snows and the spring rains, without hindrance into the farm rivulet, where they quickly flow beyond reach to the distant river. The stores of water being gone early in the summer the rivulet dries, and the stream into which it flows gets wonderfully small, and the mill stops, and on the river the boats ground.

"Ditches and drains are made to carry the water away and they do it. Ditches are the outlets, and the water will always flow away in them. To keep up a supply of moisture or of water there must be a holding back of the water. This is done in many ways, when the avenues of nature are undisturbed. On the surface it is kept in hollows or basins, where swamps and bog-holes are formed; in sloughs; in mucky land; underneath rocks; under the leaves and trees, where the sun does not cause it to evaporate. To prevent evaporation there must be coolness, and to make coolness there must be shade and humid surroundings. Under the surface it is held in pockets, in veins and subterancan places where it has washed out its own bed, and in the constant percolating and oozing out from swamps, wet places and other natural reservoirs on top of the earth. Where there is no drainage to carry the water away it fills all these fountains for the drier portions of the seasons. Each rain adds to its supply. Before there was so much drainage, water was furnished by wells of moderate depth and springs were plenty. Now permanent springs are scarce, and the old wells get dry early in the season."

Far back in our memories of childhood we retained the faintest recollection of a few lines from the pen of Dr. Benjamin Franklin, found in Poor Richard's Almanac, which would serve as a text upon which Col. Curtis might have based the above extract; yet that during the half century in which the world had moved farther on, than in any one thousand years of earth's history, foresters and farmers should have been found manifestly retrograding on this question of the world's water supply, was a mystery to us. Though we had even then begun writing out the story in briefs of our new agriculture, more than once we came near to giving up the hope of living long enough to convince the world of the efficacy of our new system. Here however was one man (Col. Curtis) at least, who had discovered the world's greatest want, and secured a hearing through the columns of the *Tribune*, speaking to hundreds of thousands of readers, and although it was the merest mention yet a beginning was secured. Just at this time also, our eldest son, Asher P. Cole, of Brooklyn N. Y., forwarded to us Mr. Stewart's work from which extracts are frequently found along the pages of this volume. Scarcely had we opened it, when the following lines attracted our attention:

"The summer rainfall in our climate is rarely, if ever, adequate to what would be a maximum crop consistent with the possibilities of the soil."

This was not news to us since we had found out that a single hill of cucumbers would drink a half barrel of water in three day's time, and having done so, would begin languishing for want of moisture, and failing to secure it, die in a week. In this connection note the amount of absorption of water by plants in the following extract from the *Country Gentleman* under the caption of "Importance of Water to Plants," which appeared subsequent to the announcement of "The New Agriculture" to the world. The italics are ours:

"In experiments performed by Sir. J. B. Lawes he found that most plants exhaled during the four or five months of their growth *more than 200 times their dry weight of water*, drawn up from the soil in which they grew. Dr. J. H. Gilbert stated that the amount of water given off by plants during growth might be approximately estimated as equal to a depth of three inches of rain for every ton of dry substance grown. Messrs. Lawes and Gilbert found by actual experiment that a crop of hay growing on land that had been manured, and giving about a ton and a half per acre, evaporated two inches more water than an unmanured crop of less than a third of a ton. These two inches were equal to 200 tons of water. A heavy crop of barley evaporated nine inches, or 1800 tons of water more than bare land lying alongside. These experiments show the *importance of underdraining so as to keep the soil pulverized and mellow, to hold like a sponge the water which falls on it, and give it off to growing plants as they need it.* A good growing crop keeps the soil in better condition than a soil without a crop, the latter being easily flooded, and again parched by drought: and without underdraining, either artificial or natural, the soil cannot be brought into a good condition to absorb and hold surplus water."

And yet, with all of this, we reasoned, the world seems to have gone stark mad in efforts to dry up and carry off the waters, acting on the theory that better crops might be thereby grown.

Though we had commenced this volume when Mr. Stewart's work came to hand, we laid by the pen, and scanned carefully everything found in Mr. Stewart's pages. It was a cornucopia of good things, the fairest, most frank and undisguised declaration of faith we had ever seen from the pen of any one writing on the subjects of irrigation and drainage. We found it invaluable. Having shown that in European countries, more especially in the British Isles, the rainfall is not only in excess of the average in America, but also that there is less of sunshine; and that the atmosphere being a humid one, evaporation is correspondingly retarded, Mr. Stewart continues:

"Our intense heats, cause a large portion of the rainfall to be evaporated directly from the soil, and our copious summer rains are seldom fully retained, but frequently in large part escape into streams and water-courses, and are lost to vegetation. Our fall, winter and early spring rains, come at times when the crops derive the least benefit, or none at all, from them. The amount of rainfall that thus escapes paying tribute to our crops is by far the largest portion of it. To estimate it at three-fourths of the whole, would not be unreasonable. There would then be left less than twelve inches of water to meet the necessities of the growing crops. That this sufficiently accounts for the low average of our yearly production of grass and grain, is not at all improbable. The supply of water then becomes the measure of the fertility of our soil, and our climate, subject to torrid drouths in the midst of the growing season, is the obstacle to success which meets the farmer, rather than the impoverished soil—a condition, indeed, mainly due to a poverty of water."

"To remove this obstacle to successful cultivation, it is only necessary that a system of irrigation be adopted. An adequate supply of water, ready for use in case of emergency, will render the farmer, the gardener, or the fruit grower, to a very large extent, independent of the vicissitudes of the season, and secure, beyond accident, a full reward for his labor. If, with a system of irrigation, a proper system of drainage be also adopted, the cultivator of the soil will have removed two adverse influences, against which he is now called upon so frequently and so ineffectually to strive."

"To irrigate economically and successfully, however, is a business which requires a large amount of technical knowledge and skill, and the expenditure of a considerable amount of capital, either in money or labor. Irrigation belongs, in fact, to a highly advanced condition of agriculture, and can only be applied to land of high value or capacity in the hands of intelligent owners."

Now, here is this eminent author of a most remarkable book, wherein is found a larger amount of research than is combined in all others on a similar subject which it has been our fortune to come across, reaching the conclusion that only by methods of irrigation and drainage successfully combined, can the former be made advantageous; and equally concluding that in this way, and this only, can anything like a full measure of production be realized;

and also, that to attempt to render lands productive to a degree of profit, not only calls for an expenditure of a considerable amount of capital, either in money or labor, but that "irrigation belongs, in fact, to a highly advanced condition of agriculture, and can only be applied to land of high value or capacity in the hands of intelligent owners."

We have alluded on previous pages to the depressions of spirit, not to say discouragements, experienced for years in pursuit of what seemed to the world a phantom. While we had found, here and there, a friend among the more eminent public men of our country, such as Hon. Warner Miller, Hon. John Sherman, Hon. Henry M. Teller, and it gives us pleasure to say, General Chester A. Arthur, who, reading patiently letters addressed to them at length upon the subject matter of our discoveries, turned away from public and private duties to give ear to what the world at large deemed an illusion—we except Hon. C. R. Earley, whose paper on fungus will be found further on in this volume, also Hon. T. L. Minier of Elmira, Hon J. H. Selkreg of Ithaca, and Hon. Augustus Frank of Warsaw—no expression could we get from anybody calculated to encourage us in the work we had undertaken. Among the above named gentlemen Senator Sherman alone was an experienced farmer. General Benjamin Butterworth, Commissioner of Patents, gave patient hearing, and reading our letters, encouraged and cheered us by pleasant words doing the heart good.

When therefore on November 29th, 1883, we received from Hon. William M. White, President at that time of our New York State Agricultural Society, a letter unreservedly endorsing our system, words fail to express the satisfaction we experienced. We had known Mr. White a lifetime, and had found him standing squarely by our side for upwards of a quarter of a century, a disciple of Horace Greeley, in advocacy and defence of the more advanced ideas of that great era. Mr. White was also the owner of a thousand acres of hard pan lands, and had stuck to them, and fortunately possesses them to-day, nor will he be likely to part with them while the work is progressing of demonstrating to the world that such lands are more valuable than any other class of soils. To this latter proposition we do not expect that the owners of bottom lands and prairies will give ready assent, but they will be forced in the end to admit the fact. To publish Mr White's letter in full, we cannot. Here, however, is an extract:

"I am happy to find you interested in making two blades of grass to grow, where but one grew before ; intent on the useful, and determined to make the hillside more productive than the valley, and what is more, by seeking a patent, inspire others to conclude, that what is worth patenting, is worth possessing. What a taking idea? "Subterranean Irrigation," an improvement on Nature's plan in Dakota's wheat fields.

"I have not a doubt that the results will prove astonishing, giving three or four feet of fertile and productive soil where only three or four inches have been hitherto realized, and placing the future of agriculture and horticulture as much ahead of the past, as thousands are ahead of hundreds.

"You say you can grow living, perpetual springs by your system of deep trenching, centering on a lower plane. I get your idea, one of reservoirs, automatic, self-acting and self-regulating, watering the other end of the grasses, feeding and watering vegetation at its roots, by inducing it to reach down for supplies of food and drink, at the same time attracting moisture and nutrition from below.

"That you are right, I know, and yet I fear you will find the average farmer, and even the most enlightened and progressive of gardeners, unprepared to accept your system as one promising profitable returns, on account of the expense incurred in fitting lands as you are doing. The silo doubles the value of the growth of an acre, and yet, so long as the old way produces meat and milk enough for the present generation, old men and young ones too, will, I fear, prefer the past to the present and future."

Upwards of two years have passed since Mr. White's letter was received, and despite the apprehensions of the author that our system may fail of early adoption, we confess to have been made happy by the knowledge, that while thousands and ten of thousands of farmers still reject ensilage, every day of our life brings evidence of the fact that the new agriculture is steadily making headway, finding friends all over the country, and that no event of the future is more certain than its general adoption. It is this general adoption which is destined to demonstrate its possibilities. Not by the trenching and fitting of five or even of ten acres can a trout stream be grown and yet, ten acres of trenching on any hillside having a firm subsoil will bring out a steady flow of crystal waters, telling the most wonderful story told since that of Moses at Horeb.

In THE AMERICAN ANGLER, of November 4th, 1884, occurred the following lines, from the pen of Mr. H. H. Thompson, an ardent student and lover of the woods and waters, and an associate of Mr. Wm. C. Harris and Seth Green, in the conduct of the above named paper:

"A new era for the brook trout is dawning. In these latter days its saviour has arisen. A remarkable man stretches forth his wand and trout streams are *created*. He smites the hillside and a purling brook or a rushing river issues in never ceasing flow from its base. He gathers the waters from the clouds, dews, and melting snows, and after their utilization in the production of marvellous results in agriculture and horticulture, releases them to form a lake of cold water absolutely pure, or a never failing crystal stream.

"Mr. A. N. Cole, of Wellsville, Allegany county, New York, has been sedulously engaged for two or three years past in developing at his "Home on the Hillside" a new system of uniform drainage, subterranean irrigation and fertilization, applicable to all mountainous, hilly or undulatory sections having a firm clay or hard-pan sub-soil. His discoveries and experiments have led to most surprising results."

Subsequent to the publication of the above, and the week previous to an address made by us at the Cooper Institute in New York City upon invitation of the Executive Committee of the Farmers' Club, of the American Institute, of New York, the following communication was published in THE AMERICAN ANGLER, under the heading of "Man Begotten Trout Streams."

*   *   *   *   *   *   *   *

"Let me state a few facts, prefacing with a statement by way of illustration. The fall of water in overflow at our village mill has been capped completely with ice, hiding the water from view, dashing down an apron at an angle of forty-five degrees or thereabouts. The Genesee, Chemung, Canisteo and Susquehanna are at many points frozen to their bottoms. Brooks issuing from springs are frozen which never within my knowledge were known to freeze before. My spring brook, evoked from our hillside, among others, has frozen in the prism of the canal into which the waters from my trenches discharge. This prism is completely filled with ice, and yet, so warm are the waters entering at the bottom of the canal, they find their way out by melting the ice above in the coldest of weather. These waters in trenches along my hillside are found in chambers of stone at a depth of about three feet and a half, covered with an earth sponge of pure mold or rich loam. There are nearly two feet of snow along my side hill on the average. Such is the effect from evaporation of the waters beneath at spring-water temperature, that the snows melt at their bottoms, and their waters, dropping down into the chambers of stone in the trenches, keep the latter full to the surface of the subsoil, and overflowing through the surface soil as though a sponge, keeping the frost out of the earth; and I find my strawberry plants growing green beneath the snow, making the white roots, etc.

"And so it is, that the deeper down the waters are dropped the warmer they become, and the deeper the snows the warmer the soil beneath them, and the more the melting at their bottoms goes on. What could be done in countries like Labrador, Alaska, Greenland, Iceland, etc., by deep trenching during their short summers, I leave to the imagination. To say the least, if they have the right kind of slopes and hillsides in Canada, if that cold country can be annexed to the United States, we will allow our neighbors of that hitherto less hospitable region to come in under our system of protection from the rule of the Frost King."

"THE ANGLER comes as a cheerful companion, pointing back to memories of youth. It is a charming paper. Long may it wave.

A. N. COLE.

Home on the Hillside, Wellsville, N. Y., March 19, 1885.

In the following quotations from our address at Cooper Union the reader will bear in mind that, on the succeeding morning, March 25th, the metropolitan press teemed with mention of Dr. Edson's report touching the impurities of the waters of the Croton. As the briefest among these editorial articles and the one coming most directly to the point, we quote from the *Sun* as follows:

"The Health Commissioners yesterday considered Dr. Edson's report of the examination which has been made of the Croton watershed, but refused to make it public. It was learned that the report speaks of the rapidly growing population of the surrounding district as a source of increasing contamination of the water supply.

"HOME ON THE HILLSIDE"

Along the Croton River and its tributaries in many places are drains which discharge their contents into the water. A condensed milk factory at Brewster's, containing 100 hands, and another at Purdy's containing 75, discharge their refuse into the water, and the offal of a slaughter house at Brewster's goes the same way. Other cases of a similar nature on a smaller scale are told of in the report."

During our remarks, we made use of the following language.

"While an attempt to trace my lines of thought, examination and investigation into the laws governing the movement of the waters over, along, through and beneath soils, ultimating at length in my discoveries, would doubtless weary my audience, I may be permitted to read the following communication made to the Farmers' Club of Elmira in confession of my obligations to that body for generous treatment received during a discussion of the merits of my system.

HOME ON THE HILLSIDE, WELLSVILLE, N.Y., JULY 31, 1884.

TO THE FARMER'S CLUB, OF ELMIRA, N. Y.

"I address you through the *Husbandman* to express my gratitude and profound appreciation of the compliments so unexpectedly paid me by a body whose proceedings I have been for years noting with deep interest.

"I have been quite generally presumed to be one who cares little for any matter outside of politics, and the tone of your expressions while discussing the question of questions with me, not merely at the present but all along through my life, touches my heart in a way I scarcely know how to sufficiently express.

"In no boastful spirit do I point to the facts connected with my lineage as found epitomized in an article in the *Free Press*, copies of which I send. From earliest childhood, two passions have seemed to rule with me, the hatred of oppression and corresponding love of liberty, and the desire to see our mother earth restored to a condition akin to the one pictured of Eden.

"Do not misunderstand me. I would not see earth made a garden by the hand of the Father, but holding as I do that work is worship, I would have the worship on the part of the children go on, till nations becoming families and families dwelling each under its own vine and fig tree, shall make home, with the farm and garden, an Eden of love the world over.

"For this disposition, and what I have done and am doing in the direction suggested, I am entitled to neither honor nor riches. Riches I have not gotten, but honor has come at last, not in the way the world counts it, as a rule. But your club seems to be impressed with the conviction that, to make money, I would not have recourse to deception. I surely would not, since I could not and be myself.

"I have, indeed, found the way to the new agriculture so fitly denominated by one of your most eminent members, Mr. C. H. Lewis. Nor the way only. Yes, I have found the thing itself, and no possible escape from it.

"If I should make money out of my discoveries it will come good, and will be used, beyond the comforts and becoming adornments of home, to do good in all ways.

"I sought the patent, not to place an embargo on the glebe, but as an incentive to improvement of the glebe.

"I was but a boy in the summer of 1838, when, amid distresses, not merely of business, but of drought almost without precedent, I travelled on foot over a large portion of Ohio, canvassing for a little horticultural and agricultural monthly, the "Buckeye Ploughboy," on more than one occasion sleeping in the open air, eating fruit by the way, and shelling out the wheat, eating it, doing the grinding with my then young and firm teeth.

"It was in the counties of Sandusky, Huron, Seneca and others of northwestern Ohio, where I found fires sweeping along the prairies and farms, destroying crops and timber, the trees having in many instances dropped their foliage before their time. Water was scarce for man and beast, and pestilence followed in the track of the droughts and desolation. Three hundred graves of fathers, mothers and children were unwet by the rains at lower Sandusky, (now Fremont). The scum upon the waters of the river was so thick that squirrels were said to have crossed it in droves without wetting their feet.

"Swamps and morasses were on fire burning to a depth, in many instances, reaching the rock from three to six feet beneath the surface, since a uniform lime-rock underlies whole counties of this portion of Ohio. It was this rock formation that especially attracted my attention. To obtain water from wells was stubborn work. Great streams in some instances gushed out in copious flow, but disappeared quickly as some deep fissure in the rock was reached in the flow of their waters.

"Thus early did I begin the observation and study of soils. Not merely did I seek to know the surface. In streams, dry in their beds, and in furrows of field and farm my studies went on. The subsoils were especially observed.

"Whence came the waters? These I knew dropped down from the clouds in the form of rains, dews, frosts and snows. When it came winter, I found out the treasures of the hail. I looked back longingly during nearly a year of dreary discontent to the leeks and onions, rains and dews and even the drifting snows of that Allegany of nearly fifty years ago. I remembered the crystal waters of the good-bye land I had left for the attractions of the then great west, and dreamed dreams of grasses all green in their verdure and grateful in their juices.

"This is a goodly land, I said mentally, and yet, without water it seems much like a place we read about, in no sense attractive. There was no end to my dreams. How can these great seams in the rocks be sealed? was the question uppermost in my mind. These streams so abundant in flow along smooth rocky channels, I said mentally, in spring and autumn, are fearful to contemplate as found amid the fervors of the summer solstice. Great rains would come in ordinary seasons, lasting at times for days in midsummer, and in three days time no desert was ever more dry. Here, in favorable seasons, was grown that wonderful white wheat we used to see in our boyhood, eclipsing that, if possible, grown in the valley of the far-famed Genesee.

"This was the school, added to a few lessons learned in Michigan, then just admitted into our Union as a state, where I studied geology and geography, physics, physiology, botany and other sciences without number in their application to the constitutions of men and animals, plants, trees, grasses, grains and all else of life in its multitudinous forms and phases.

"And all along since I have studied on, and reached conclusions and demonstrated them as follows:—

"1. The Father gives us the rains and dews and frozen waters in copious abundance, nor need any of the sons and daughters of men, nor beasts of the field, or fowl, or fish, or flesh in any form, nor so much as the grass beneath our feet want for food and drink.

"2. Man, made but little lower than the angels, and monarch as he is of earth, has the ability to gather up the waters in store to be used as wanted, controlling their flow as they make their ways adown to the seas, and in facile direction so conduct them in currents as to make their tracks the ways of pleasantness and paths of peace, at the same time furnishing fruitions to earth's inhabitants in basket and store of measureless abundance.

"In the discussions indulged in on the part of your Club at date of July 26th, while considering the systems of horticulture and agriculture, proposed by your correspondent, the question unanswered was the one always asked 'will it pay?'

"That a body of men like yours should have been found in substance agreeing to every proposition I make in urging the merits of my system, and that, too, when that system proposes the most startling of new departures, is evidence that the world has reached a point where all things seem possible with men as with their Maker. Reading your discussions as I do, you agree to this:—

"1. The rains and dews and melting snows can be gathered into store, and in regions of country where hard-pan and clay subsoils are found, so held back or allowed to flow on as to feed and water vegetation in their track, giving to all trees, plants, grasses, grains and other forms of plant life what is needed by way of food and drink in abundance, and never in surfeit.

"2. You agree that the waters moving evenly and in uniform currents from mountain and hilltop along slopes and inclines till the streams are reached, passing through the soil in subterranean flow, bear with them nutrition for plants at their roots, which, by capillary attraction are watered and fed in conformity to the necessities of each and all.

"3. You equally agree that irrigation and abundant supply of food being realized, all forms of plant growth will be perfectly developed.

"4. Again, you agree that when my system comes to be generally adopted, there will be fewer floods, fewer frosts of a deadly character, and as for droughts they need not occur in regions of country at least underlaid with the prevailing subsoil of the slopes and inclines of the Southern Tier, and of other regions similarly conformed.

"By way of encouragement, let me say therefore, that the conclusions which seem to have been reached by your club are those arrived at by Hon. William M. White, President of our State Agricultural Society, Hon. Warner Miller, Chairman of the Committee on Agriculture of the United States Senate, General Benjamin Butterworth, Commissioner of Patents, Hon. Henry M. Teller, Secretary of the Interior, and, if I am correctly informed, Hon. Geo. B. Loring, Commissioner of Agriculture, and hundreds of others, as eminent in all ways as the most notable in our land.

"In conclusion, let me say that, all I have claimed can be done, and most of it has been done and demonstrated by myself; the results are so wonderful in all ways as to incline me to shrink from their enumeration and specification, and yet here is an epitome.

"Waters having descended their incline, however impregnated or discolored at their sources, reach the level of the streams in purity, having left all behind in their track adapted to the development of plant growth.

"The stones, sticks and all else in the soil inducing fungus growths at the roots of plants being removed and placed deep down in the trenches, and manures having been so composted with lime, ashes, salts and other fermentizing and assimilating agencies as to prevent germination of seeds, and completely destroying the seed of fungus, every root of every plant will be free from disease, and perfect stalks, buds, blossoms and fruit follow, and health coming at all stages of growth, it is transmitted beyond to the consumer not merely, but to the seeds and germinations of future plant growths.

"Stagnation of waters nowhere occurring, health rather than decay and death will be found in the track of the waters. The potatoe rot will be conquered, wire worms and the small grub eating the white roots of vegetation will largely if not wholly disappear, and when it comes to malaria with all of its animalcule "in the air above, the earth beneath, and the waters under the earth," these will in their baneful infections pass away.

"Among our hills and mountains, springs will gush out in purity and permanency, lakes be begotten, rivers formed, and reservoirs be found where none have hitherto been seen ; and these, swarming with fish, will so multiply the food products of land and water and so improve them in flavor and quality, as to eclipse anything realized in the past.

"But this applies only to lands such as are found in the region round about us and to similar subsoils elsewhere.

"On nearly all portions of the world, outside of sea levels, by the use of tile and kindred appliances in the form of troughs on the elevations and slopes in which to aggregate the waters, all of which are provided for under our system, the retention of water beneath the soil in its flow along declines in subterranean currents, evaporation through the earth sponge being uniform and inspiring, the climates of New Jersey and Long Island, if not of Delaware and Maryland, will come to New York and New England.

"Will it pay? I answer: Come one, come all to our "Home on the Hillside" and see for yourselves. My neighbors have seen, tested, feasted and felt, and my work is before their eyes. Some of your own citizens know and realize what I have demonstrated and accomplished."

The balance of my address at the Cooper Union in New York, will be found in the following article from THE AMERICAN ANGLER as reported by its Managing Editor Mr. Wm. C. Harris, who was present on the occasion ; it appeared under the heading of "The Waters Led Captive."

"On Tuesday last, March 24, Mr. A. N. Cole, of Wellsville, Allegany County, N. Y., addressed, by invitation, the Farmer's Club of the American Institute, at their semi-monthly meeting, on the subject of his 'New Agriculture.' He took his audience by storm, nearly or quite every person present pronouncing his address one of the most striking ever delivered before that body; convincing, apparently, his hearers that he had found out the way to grow springs, spring brooks, lakes and rivers of water, going to the clouds for sources of supply and gathering in the rains, dews and waters from melting snows, 'holding, husbanding and housing' them at will, and moving them forward in a way to produce such results in agriculture and horticulture as to astonish everyone in this age of marvels.

"Mr. Cole denominated his servant (the waters) "Leviathan," declared he had him yoked, a hook in his jaw, and proposed to plow with him until paradise lost shall be regained. The people who are just at present not only vexed in spirits about a plentiful supply of Croton, but are fearful that our water is being poisoned by surface washings, will, we feel sure, read with interest the conclusion of Mr. Cole's address, as follows:

"And now, ladies and gentlemen, having extended to me a patient and attentive hearing, for which thanking you once more, permit me in closing to say that I have been engaged for three or four years in demonstrating the use to be made of the waters, and have become convinced that by gathering them in and directing their flow in subterranean currents they may be dropped deeply enough into reservoirs along inclines to hold them not only in reserve, but at a temperature considerably above freezing, keeping frost out of the soil. To say the least, in moderate winter weather, by evaporation through the soil, the snows will be melted at their bottoms, and the waters dropping into the reservoirs below, their movement will follow in even flow through surface soils, as through a sponge, and through subsoils in percolation, bearing with them inspirations to plant growth, having an influence as yet scarcely dreamed of.

"It is not only subsurface, subterranean or underground irrigation which is realized in perfection under operation of the methods governing in my system, but a perfect method of drainage also, carrying off the surplus waters and leaving to mother earth the work of elaboration, and to plants their selections of food and desired fill of drink, always in abundance, and never in surfeit.

"The time has come when around and about every home of our entire land the work should begin of subsurface or underground irrigation and drainage. If on slopes and inclines, with firm subsoils and an abundance of stone, the work can be readily and economically done. If the soils are porous, then should clay or cement be used in construction of reservoirs and inclines, and the form of tile, to which recourse may be had, has only to be shaped for the work in hand, when yoking of "Leviathan" will be begun in a way to demonstrate what he is capable of doing.

"Suffice it to say that were the slopes on the east and west banks of the Hudson thus generally trenched and fitted, your great and grand river would show a steady current of pure spring water moving down to the ocean, regardless of droughts or removal of the forests, so defying diminution of its tides as to make navigation of any portion of its channel, even in midsummer, a something unnecessary to provide otherwise for. You will find the begetting of lakes at any altitude chosen among the mountains, hills and valleys of the counties of Albany, Columbia, Schenectady, Schoharie, Montgomery, Herkimer, Dutchess, Putnam, Greene and Ulster, not to mention others farther north, not only a pastime but a profit, of which not one in a million of the American people yet dream. You will find that growing of crystal springs, and begetting of rivulets and rivers of water is a something as easy of accomplishment as the sinking of a well, or of an ordinary cistern.

"You will find the grasses of your dooryards and lawns and the plants in your gardens greenly growing and making root all winter beneath the snows; and the snows melting at their bottoms, the waters will find their way to bases of slopes at temperature several degrees above freezing. You will find water, evolved on and out from your lakes, hung up along your hillsides sufficient to provide all of reserve needed to hold the Hudson at high tide during every month of the year; and, applying like principles to what has been denominated the Great American desert, you will see gathered in those torrents of water continually descending the slopes of the Sierras and Rockies, coming of melting snows and passing on from trench to trench, borne down mountain sides, across plain, and descending into valleys, nowhere appearing on the surface, except as man may direct, making confluence with the rivers in purity and perpetuity of flow.

"You will find surface and subsoils alike made softer, more porous and spongy, alkali extracted or again infused, salts, ammonia, etc., evenly diffused, fertilization perfected, and production increased to a degree beyond computation. You will find hundreds, yea, thousands of trees growing, giving shade and bearing fruits to where one is being felled by the woodman's axe, and clouds forming and rains and dews descending in hitherto rainless and treeless regions. The English grasses, growing greenly all over our southland amid the fervors of the summer solstice, will give to our brethren of that section the milk and honey, butter and cheese, and other like products of our graver north lands. By way of experiment, try this method on the dooryards, lawns, gardens, etc., about your houses, and let your city fathers look into it and make up their minds to have babbling brooks, with occasional cascades, dropping waters crystal-clear into miniature lakes of the parks and places already existing, and steadily multiplying, in and about New York, Brooklyn and other towns in circuit, and see what will come of it. Lest " Leviathan " be underrated as regards his powers, let lakes everywhere be hung up among the rocks and mountains of New England, and, by use of the water motor, let the wheels moving the mills, factories, foundries and workshops of that region be run under the force and impulse of his self-begotten, automatic, self-regulating, unfed, unwatered, yoked, tamed and magic movements—*and so shall the harvest be.*"

The following discussion of our system by the Farmer's Club of Elmira, N. Y., occurred at a meeting on July 26, 1885, and was fully reported in the columns of *The Husbandman* of Elmira, from which it is now transcribed :

" In the discussion of the subject of Mr. Cole's system by the Farmer's Club of Elmira, at its weekly meeting of July 26th, the following report published in *The Husbandman*, demonstrates the interest manifested in it :

" On the call for correspondence the Secretary read a letter describing a new system of irrigation. Although it had not been addressed directly to the Club, and the writer perhaps had no thought that it would be submitted for discussion, it seemed pertinent, and, in fact, was invited by members to whom a synopsis had been given, and they gave attentive hearing during the reading, for the matters presented were calculated to excite interest in the minds of farmers whose hill lands of obstinate soil and under ordinary treatment failed to give due returns for labor expended in fitting them for grain and grass crops. The first expressions were by gentlemen who had personal acquaintance with Mr. Cole, and who evinced pleasure in testifying to his worth as a citizen and his high sense of honor. They believe he would not lay before the people a scheme to defraud a single farmer, no matter how much profit he might reap from the transaction. Mr. Lewis was particularly warm in his expressions of regard, and referring to matters embraced in the letter he said :

"'We all know that it is possible to increase crops four-fold by irrigation, taking as the standard the average yields on lands that are subject to extremes of drought and wet, and our clay lands are nearly all of this character. I have seen an illustration on my own land of the principle embraced in Mr. Cole's system where a ridge held an accumulation of water from rains until it could slowly pass through and furnish moisture for plants growing below. Their growth was two or three times as great as on other portions of the field of like character where moisture was not provided at the right time. If we can, by any system, hold back the surplus water that comes from rains and snows,—water that usually runs over the surface to the nearest creek or river—and let it out just at the time when the plants need it, I am confident that we can reap harvests uniform in excellence and always full. The question to be considered is—can we afford to inaugurate the system and carry it to completion when its cost will add greatly to the investment, making the farm cost, let us say, twice as much as before the improvement? I think the expense may be afforded with proper management, and that its gradual improvement, so that a piece of land treated by this system may give profits to be applied to the improvement of more land. If we were required to treat our hillsides in the way proposed all at once, there is not money enough in this county to effect the improvement, but with a very small part of the money that would be required to do the whole work we can begin and then use the profits to carry forward the work. I believe the time is coming, and is not far distant, when the face of the earth will be changed and a new agriculture, more profitable than ours, will be open to every farmer. I believe the ingenuity of man will devise ways by which every acre that we now cultivate will be made to produce two or three times as much as we get from it now. That will be our new agriculture. Perhaps this system discovered by Mr. Cole is the first step toward the general improvement.

"G. S. McCann. If we can adopt any plan that will increase crops to two or three times present yield we can afford considerable expense to effect the improvement. It is not so much a matter of cost in the outset as returns afterwards.

"W. A. Armstrong. That is the right way to view the new system. First, ascertain by actual inspection of the grounds treated by Mr. Cole two or three years ago what improvement is effected, what advantage is already seen; in fact, get full information from every available source. Now suppose his estimate of cost be taken at $200 or $250 to the acre. Manifestly it will not be within the range of possibilities for farmers generally to improve fifty or a hundred acres in a single season at such great cost. But take another view, premising of course that benefits received will repay the outlay. Take one acre and treat it by this system. Suppose its profits in annual crops are one-fifth of the cost required to provide irrigation. Why plainly in five years the profit will provide funds for treating another acre. Then there will be two acres to yield profits, and accumulation of gain would, in a few years, provide for treating an extensive field. Sometimes it is advantageous for farmers to lay out a good deal of money in improvements, even when the money must be borrowed. As for instance suppose a field never does more than return cost of labor expended on it. The land may have cost a hundred dollars an acre, but if it will produce nothing more than fair compensation for labor employed on it, the value is nothing, because the labor can be sold for the money without waiting for crops to grow, or it might be employed on other portions of the farm where it would secure fuller returns. But if this field, by a proper system of improvement can be made to pay a large profit, not only on the money expended in improvement but on the original cost of the land, and also on the labor employed in cultivation, why, to the dullest mind the argument in favor of making the improvement will be very plain. That there are such fields on a great majority of our hill farms, there can be no doubt. When we find the new agriculture, of which Mr. Lewis speaks, we shall find these lands improved by some system and the gain to farmers who now own them will be very great.

"C. H. Lewis. That is precisely what I am looking for. My farm is mainly heavy soil that has cost a great deal of labor to bring to its present condition where some profit can be derived by cultivation. But developement is not completed. I suppose that after all the years I have spent in trying to improve my farm it may be worth $50 per acre. Now if it could be improved by Mr. Cole's plan, as I believe it might, it would bring better profits on $500 per acre than it does now on $50. If this supposition be correct it would be wise economy to expend a large sum of money on every acre to bring it to the highest state of production. I dare say that $100 or $200 expended on an acre might, in the course of eight or ten years, put into my pocket a great deal larger sum of profit than I can have by cultivating the land as it now is, and the gain after the original cost is returned, would be all profit."

The foregoing is only a portion of the discussion upon the occasion, the members participating in it being its President, Mr. Cann, its Secretary, Mr. Armstrong, Editor of the *Husbandman* and others, several of the number being among the first farmers of the Chemung Valley. Such was the tone of the discussion throughout as to cheer our heart and strengthen our determination to speak out boldly, and tell what we had found out. This we began doing, and yet, so startling were our statements, and so far short had we yet come of a satisfactory demonstration, that we went slowly, proceeding step by step, fortifying as we progressed. Not all of the members of our family, nor so much as a single individual among our more intimate neighbors and friends were able to understand us, so complete was the revolution impending. Then too, we may as well confess it, faithful friends never before doubting, felt that we were deceiving ourself, over confident, and were spending money in a way that would never return. That our credit correspondingly suffered is a fact we may as well confess.

At this juncture, through the kind consideration of President Arthur and the Hon. Henry M. Teller, Secretary of the Interior, both of whom had know us a lifetime and had taken a deep interest in our discoveries, we received a commission sending us to the Pacific Coast, to examine the last completed link of the Northern Pacific Railroad. This, though helping to the extent of less than a thousand dollars, came at the time most needed, enabling us to go forward with the work of demonstration. Before going on our official western visit, we assured the President and Secretary that we had no doubt whatever that such were the nature of our discoveries, that were our system to be applied to the reclamation of the lands belonging to the government in that desolate region denominated the Great American desert, these could be made as generally productive as those of other sections of our country, now thickly populated, and in certain portions, vastly more productive. Going out, and returning, we were convinced, beyond the shadow of a doubt that millions of acres of the lands skirting that greatest of lines. the Northern Pacific Railway, as seen along mountain sides, plateaus, plains and valleys found in treeless and rainless regions could be completely reclaimed, and made as fertile and productive as those of the most favored countries of earth.

Reaching home, about the tenth of May 1884, all went hopefully on for a while, till came that fearful blizzard, not soon to be forgotten, about the last of the month, and so chilling our expectations as to bring us near to discouragement. It was while journeying to the Pacific coast that we had occasion for a few hours to look squarely in the face a champion blizzard, gotten up at Manitoba's best, leaving no room for doubt as regards the place where, congelation putting on the intense, "the frozen waters gendered are." Whether the one which struck western New York and other sections in the East and West on the 29th of May, 1884, has been equalled in the memory of the oldest inhabitant is doubtful. No more decisive test of the efficacy of our system as protection against frost could have been applied. The ground was frozen to the depth of from one to two inches on all plowed lands upon our fifty acres outside of the acre and a quarter at that time perfected in trenching under our system. In the latter, evaporation of spring water through the soil was such as to prevent freezing, and the damage to our garden was correspondingly mitigated. Our strawberries were much injured by the frost striking the buds and blossoms, and the currants were killed at the tops but not at the bottoms of the bushes. The result was, damage, but by no means that total loss of the crops experienced by farmers and gardners in western New York generally. This convinced us that our system is proof against the effects of frost to a degree that makes it, in this particular, worth millions annually to regions subject to disaster from this source.

It was a consolation to know that our system had proven in some degree protective against Manitoba's champion blizzard, and yet, in view of the fact that we had gotten up great expectations, confident of being able to show to the world the wonder workings of our system to an extent coming so near to demonstration as to make our way clear to immediate success, such were the effects of frost upon our grounds as to cause us to feel that we wished nobody to come and see till another season. Many came, nevertheless during the summer, and in no instance did anyone go away unconvinced. Individuals came without number, chief among them being Mr. J. Austin Shaw of Rochester, and Mr. D. C. Hopkins, of the Almond Fruit Farm, both saying pleasant things and doing all that was possible to cheer and encourage us to perseverance in the work we had undertaken. In the meantime, a few brave men among our Allegany county farmers, having organized a club, had so far gotten a start with their organization as to make themselves felt all over our county. Discussion of the merits of our system had begun in a lively way, the news getting out that our patent had been allowed. The good effects were immediate, prompting the Allegany Farmers' Club to appoint a committee to visit our grounds, and examine into the merits of our system. The committee came, and after spending several hours in examining into our work and noting results, reached conclusion as follows:

WELLSVILLE, Aug. 11, 1884.

MR. A. N. COLE:

The undersigned committee, representing the Farmers' Club of Allegany county, having examined the plot of ground fitted under your improved system of subterranean drainage, irrigation and fertilization, take pleasure in assuring the public that our observations justify us in concluding that you are enabled to realize all you claim to accomplish by that system.

E. E. HYDE, Belmont,	JAS. S. WILCOX, Belmont,
C. A. WINDUS, "	J. P. TRUMAN, "
D. H. NORTON, Friendship.	

This committee was as ably constituted as any one of equal number that could be chosen from the membership of any like organization in our State. Two of them, to wit : Messrs. Truman and Hyde being physicians, while Messrs, Wilcox, Windus and Norton are among the most successful of Allegany farmers, the latter at this time President of the county club. Hon. B. F. Langworthy, widely known in Allegany and adjoining counties as a gentleman of rare enterprise and intelligence, one of the most substantial and successful of Allegany farmers, came about the same time, and making careful examination, pronounced the new agriculture the way to success. It was the year before, that Mr. J. F. Langworthy came, and about the same time also Mr. D. C. Hopkins, of the Almond Fruit Farm, both of whom formed favorable conclusions touching the influence of subsurface irrigation on fruit trees, as shown by the single apple tree left standing on our grounds at the time trenching was begun.

On the first of July, 1885, the "Home on the Hillside" was visited by Dr. J. P. Roberts, now of Ithaca, N. Y., who has in charge the University Farm, at Cornell, N. Y., an agriculturist having a national reputation. Layman, as we are, though having faith amounting to sight in our system, we felt nevertheless, a trifle anxious lest this most eminent of farm doctors might discover defects in our system as to the conformation of soils, methods of fertilizing, or in other particulars of a serious nature, hence we were especially gratified, when he uttered his opinion as follows :

"Yes, Mr. Cole, you do all you claim to accomplish; you gather the waters into your reservoirs and pass them through the soil rather than leaving them to run riot along the surface; you transform this hitherto shunned and dreaded hardpan into soft, porous, productive and best of soils to the depth of your trenches, thereby enabling the roots of vegetation to descend deeply into the earth. You remove the stone operating as obstructions and diseasing the roots of plants, and put them where they will do most good; you pro-

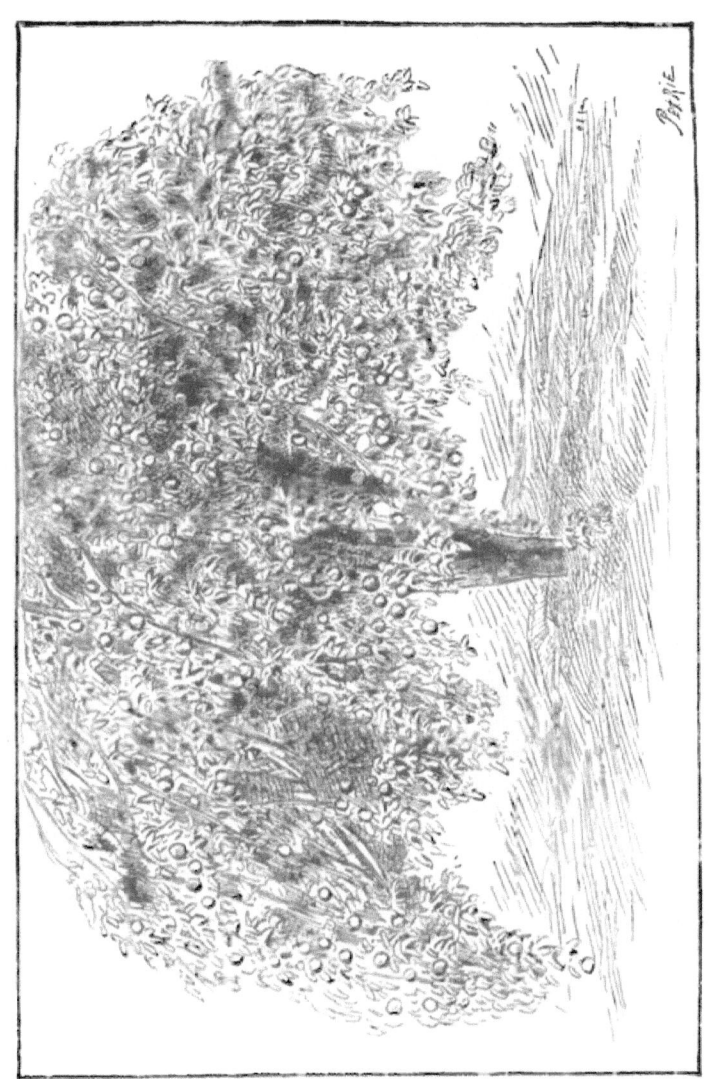

THE OLD APPLE TREE.

vide against floods and droughts, and to a great extent, if not wholly, defeat the effects of frost, but in doing this, it seems to me that you are digging your trenches much wider than necessary, and it would be better to sink them deeper, thus avoiding unnecessary cost, and at the same time making warm, soft, porous and productive soil to greater depth."

In discussing this point, the Professor told a story of his experience while in Iowa of tracing the roots of clover in their descent in a gravel bank, beating the one told us by Horace Greeley as regarded the descent of the roots of trees to a depth of twenty-two feet to reach the waters of a river in subterranean flow. Mr. Greeley made his statement as one of information and belief, coming from credible witnesses in California, while Professor Roberts based his statement upon personal knowledge of the fact that, in order to reach water, clover roots descended to a depth of either eight or eighteen feet. (We are quite sure it was the latter depth but as we may have misunderstood him, we will therefore refer the public to the author of this last story to say whether it was eight or eighteen feet that the clover roots found their way into the earth.) Whether eight, or eighteen, it is safe to conclude that the tops of that clover corresponded to the length and strength of the roots. Having settled this point, every reader will not fail to discover the reason why there is now growing and ripening in our garden in boundless profusion more bushels of luscious strawberries to the acre than the average farmer grows of potatoes, and that these are in hundreds of instances, the size of ordinary peaches. Considerable numbers of these berries measure from four to eight inches in circumference. We have decided, as suggested by Dr. Roberts, to go down a little deeper, sinking our trenches from three to four feet into the subsoil, and arranging all overflow trenches beneath the surface soil out of reach of the deepest spading or plowing.

A memorable day was the 7th of July, 1885, the one upon which occurred the formal introduction of our system to the world. We are now writing at the date of August 3rd, 1885. On Wednesday, July 30th, Mr. William C. Harris, Editor in Chief of the AMERICAN ANGLER, published at 252 Broadway, New York City, made us a visit. He spent a day with us, looking over our system in detail and gave decision as follows : " The New Agriculture " is the way to a new earth with pure waters and healthy plants and peoples," adding "Brothers Cole and Thompson are right about it, the brook trout *must* not go, and *will* not go."

Below will be found an extract from the correspondence of the *Buffalo Express*, second in circulation and influence to no paper in our State outside of the metropolis, it appearing on the day succeeding our exhibit, July 8th.

" Yesterday was a notable day for Wellsville, or at least for one of its most widely-known inhabitants. Nestled away among the ragged Allegany hills, this snug town of about 4,000 people has in common with the rest of the world, its ambitions and its celebrities. The particular industry that yesterday took a long stride toward popular recognition and favor is one growing up on the western hill of the town, and is known as Cole's system of underground irrigation. Reckoned either as a freak or curiosity, or better than both of these, as a step into the next century in the domain of agriculture, this little plot of five acres of land, only two of which are as yet developed, will bear the closest inspection of either the skeptic or the willing convert.

" But perhaps everybody is not aware of the system, now under practical trial, which promises to revolutionize the world's agriculture, nay, according to its enthusiastic author, has already done so. Some four years ago Mr. A. N. Cole, better known as the "father of the Republican party" and the veteran editor of the Wellsville

Free Press, began to put in operation a system of agriculture based on underground irrigation, an idea entirely his own. He had been studying the system a number of years before that time, but had not until then carried it into practice. There were drawbacks that need not be mentioned here and there was, of course, a town full of people who laughed at the idea as a crazy notion sure to come to nothing. But Mr. Cole persevered, and it is safe to say that yesterday he was able to demonstrate his success so entirely as to ensure him the title of the proudest man in western New York and perhaps out of it as well."

From beginning to end of a two column article, commendatory throughout, the correspondent of *The Express* drew a faithful picture of what he saw on this occasion.

We now give the report of Mr. Charles A. Green, sent to our place as special correspondent of the New York *Tribune*. In making the report Mr. Green dates his letter at Clifton, July 8th, on the day succeeding our exhibition:

"A short ride from Rochester up the Genesee Valley among promising grain fields, fragrant meadows and shady pastures, and another hour along the southern tier bring me to a prosperous, hill-girt village, lying like a speckled egg in a bird's nest. In this pretty village of Wellsville is the home of Mr. A. N. Cole, the veteran editor and horticultural experimenter. His residence is situated on an eastern slope commanding views of the village and surrounding country. I found here a company of about 100 gentlemen, ministers, politicians, physicians, the press and neighbors, who, like *The Tribune* correspondent, had been invited to witness the results of 'The New Agriculture," as Mr. Cole has named his new method of irrigation. Mr. Cole expressed his pleasure at seeing *The Tribune* represented, and remarked that it was Horace Greeley who gave him his first insight into this method of agriculture, by relating the peculiarities of a section of country in California. Near Los Angeles a river disappeared from view and followed a subterranean course for a distance of twenty-two miles on an average of twenty feet below the surface of the soil. The land surrounding this portion of country was a desert, but that immediately over the subterranean river was covered with luxurious vegetation. He also spoke of a similar mysterious disappearance of a river in the Mesilla Valley, New Mexico. It was the knowledge of these lost rivers, he said, that gave birth to the ideas which have grown into "The New Agriculture." In speaking of the remarkable growth over these rivers, Mr. Greeley mentioned the fact that vegetables and trees growing there, sent their roots down until they reached the river water beneath. Mr. Cole says that Professor Roberts, of Ithaca, has told him that he has traced red clover roots to a depth of eighteen feet, that were growing in a bed of gravel overlying water.

"Mr. Cole has been studying irrigation since he was seventeen years old, but his present system flashed upon him within the past few years. He has not yet extended his working model over more than two to three acres. I shall attempt to explain what I saw, and to state the claims of Mr. Cole as clearly as I can, considering our brief and frequently interrupted conversation.

"We were first shown a patch of strawberries containing nearly two acres. These plants were grown in hills about eighteen inches apart each way, mulched with forest leaves, liberally fertilized with yard manure, and irrigated after the new method. I was told by the former owner of the hillside that when he sold it to Mr. Cole it was an unproductive piece of ground. The soil proper was not over ten or twelve inches deep and rested upon a tenacious, clayey hard-pan, which was impervious to water. He said the frosts acted so seriously upon this soil, on account of the surplus water not being able to escape through the subsoil that it was almost impossible to keep plants alive in it during winter. Even the fence posts would be thrown out by the frost in a very short time. A prominent contractor who was walking by my side at the time, said that all that section of the country was underlaid by this peculiar subsoil, which is a great drawback to plant growth. I was also informed by this same gentleman that this part of Allegany County was not favorable for strawberry growing, or other fruit except apples, and that the supply of small fruits is received largely from other sections. Mr. Cole has planted numerous varieties of strawberries upon his side hill, among which I recognized the Bidwell, Sharpless, and other familiar varieties. The fruit was of an astonishing size and grew in great abundance. While I live in a strawberry country, and am myself a strawberry grower, I cannot remember when I have seen so fine a display of strawberries growing upon the vines as I saw here. There were, however, evidences of high culture. A gentleman by my side echoed my sentiments by remarking that we could increase the size of fruits in our own gardens by such thorough cultivation as this. I regretted that Mr. Cole did not have a plot of strawberries growing near by which did not receive any benefit from his method of irrigation, for then we could have compared results. Adjoining the strawberries were growing different kinds of garden crops, also currants, raspberries, blackberries, potatoes and a few fruit trees. At one point, where the ground was terraced, I noticed, growing on the ragged edge a row of onions. I called attention to the fact that while these onions were on the very brink, there was no indication of their being disturbed by washing of the soil, as might have been expected in such a position. In fact everything showed that in no place had the rainfall run down the surface as ordinarily, to the detriment of anything growing thereon as the water passed into the drains underlying." * * *

Mr. Green's article covers a full column and a half of *The Tribune*, and is remarkably conservative in tone from first to last, written by a manifestly level-headed and even-handed man, but one nevertheless coming wholly unprepared for what he saw. Himself an extensive gardener, fruit grower and nursery man at Rochester, the Flower City, where gardens and gardening form a distinguishing feature of business, and coming, as he did, out of that far-famed delta of the Genesee, (which is ordinarily exempt from frost, a fortnight earlier in Spring, and three or four weeks later in Autumn than other sections of western New York) to find at Wellsville near the source of the Genesee River, the climate of Delaware and Maryland, not to say of the Virginias, growing fruits and vegetables superior in flavor, and immeasurably prolific of yield. Fair minded and just, his summing up as follows need not be wondered at.

"The correspondent of *The Tribune* was asked on every hand, "What do you think of this 'New Agriculture?'" I reply frankly that, while I consider that Mr. Cole claims too much, there appears to be in it much that is novel and useful. Others who try similar experiments in different soils and locations may not be able to obtain such results. I do not doubt that an acre of ground can be made to yield an increased harvest by the new method, but whether it is a paying investment is another question, and would depend upon circumstances. For high gardening, near large cities, where the subsoil is tenacious, it would doubtless be profitable. For general field culture of common farm crops, I should hesitate to recommend it until I had investigated further, owing to the great expense to be incurred."

That the editors of *The Tribune* were unprepared for even so favorable a report as this, is evidenced by the following, appearing on the editorial page of that paper at date of July 14th.

"Those who have read that most suggestive of all American books on agriculture, "What I Know of Farming,"—will be interested in the account in another column which Mr. Charles A. Green, the well-known horticulturist and nurseryman of Rochester, gives of some novel experiments in irrigation by Mr. Cole, of Wellsville. The foundation of the new agriculture is subterranean irrigation by a system of drains, which being kept supplied with water, in turn afford a permanent supply of moisture ready to be taken up by the plant growth above as fast as it is needed. There are other principles involved, but this is the main one, and Mr. Cole claims that his system will produce ten tons of hay to the acre, or 300 bushels of strawberries, etc., and thus yield a profitable return on the money expended. It will be noted that while Mr. Green does not indorse these claims he thinks that the result of the experiment at Wellsville are remarkable and worthy of attention."

Eminent among editors who came on this day was Mr. R. S. Lewis of the *Progressive Batavian*, published at Batavia, Genesee County, N. Y., from whose report it would be impossible to make extracts and do justice either to its author or to the public, and therefore we copy nearly all of it.

'Mr. Cole's farm consists of five acres of what was, four years ago, and a part of which is now, a sterile hillside of clayey soil so poor as to grudgingly yield sufficient substance to grow field daisies. It is as steep as the steepest part of Burleigh hill Pavillion, the Bethany hill just east of the Centre, or any other hill in Genesee county of which we have any knowledge; and as to its ever becoming profitably productive, we don't believe there is a foot of land in all our county which was equally unpromising. Some thirty years ago Mr. Cole conceived the idea that plant life might be greatly, almost immeasurably, stimulated by underground irrigation. He had neither time nor opportunity then to perfect and test his thought, but it continued to simmer through him and to recall itself to his attention again and again as the years passed on.

"His conviction on the matter was greatly strengthened and stimulated by a conversation with Mr. Horace Greeley, in which that gentleman told him what he had heard of the wondrous productiveness near Los Angeles, California, where vegetation was fed by a subterranean river. Mr. Cole had thought and investigated until he had no doubt about the fact of a theory, but how to accomplish the irrigation—how to make his thought practical, was the question.

"At last how to do it dawned suddenly upon him—the mists of questionings and doubts were gone—his dream of the years had materialized—his vision was clear. Where could he better test and demonstrate the truth and value of his discovery than on his own sterile, unpromising hillside. Along its eastern front runs a highway with wayside gutter adjoining his land. Parallel with this, and some forty to fifty feet apart, and across about half his land to its highest boundary, he caused a series of trenches about two and a half feet wide by four and a half to five feet deep to be dug, and filled to within eighteen inches of the surface with coarse large stone covered with loose flat stone, for subterranean water reservoirs. These reservoirs were connected by numerous shallow and smaller trenches partially filled with small stones at about eighteen inches from the surface and designed to carry off from trench to trench all surplus water. After the laying of the stone all the trenches, little and big, are covered with straw or litter of any kind, as in ordinary ditching, and then covered with dirt. Thus each large trench is a reservoir capable of holding from three to three and a half feet of water through its entire length before it reaches the height where carried off by the cross trenches. The water from the rains and melting snows instead of passing off in surface rills and channels is caught in these reservoirs and slowly and continuously filters through the soil from trench to trench—sweats through it, so to speak—rendering it porous, pliable, spongy—always sufficiently damp to feed and stimulate vegetation to the highest degree, and yet always sufficiently dry to be in the best possible order for cultivation.

"On a part of his plantation which Mr. Cole has thus treated he last year cut three crops of timothy grass, each crop being in the head when cut. Most of the trenched ground is now planted with blackberry and raspberry bushes and strawberry vines. What the berry bushes will do yet is only conjectural—they have a strong, healthy, prominent development—but the strawberry vines—it is utterly impossible to appropriately describe their wonderous wealth of productiveness. The vines are literally loaded with berries and their average size is marvelous. Many were readily found which measured nearly eight inches in circumference, and there were no small berries. Mr. Cole proudly said : 'I have berries this year as big as peaches,' and, he confidently added, 'I will grow them next year as large as apples.' He claimed he would this year harvest more bushels of strawberries from his vines than any farmer would grow bushels of potatoes from the same area of ground. He said the cost of putting his ground in its present condition of reservoirs and consequent productiveness was about $500 per acre, and he expected to realize $1,200 from his strawberry crop alone this year.

"One or two facts more are worthy of mention, 1st—While the ground all around this plot was last winter frozen several feet deep, this ground was not frozen—the plants grew the winter through. 2d—One of the deluge rains so prevelant this season poured down upon Wellsville a few days since, and while the hillsides all around were furrowed and ditched by the running waters, this plot was not washed in the least—the torrents sank into its porous soil, were caught in its reservoirs and the surplus passed off through its transverse trenches without in the least disturbing its surface or the crops grown thereon.

"Brother Cole claims that by his 'New Agriculture' every kind of vegetable production can be increased from five to ten fold,—that by it men could realize more from five or ten acres, and with less labor too, than they now do from farms of hundreds of acres—that this fact will become rapidly apparent—that 'The New Agriculture, something the world has never seen or realized before has been discovered and will prevail.' If it shall in any measure fulfill its early promise as shown in Mr. Cole's small experiment then it ought to and will prevail. Some wise man has remarked, 'He who causes two blades of grass to grow where only one grew before, is a benefactor of his race' or words to that effect, and for what his new idea has already established we have no hesitation in saying Mr. Cole is entitled to honor and esteem as a public benefactor. His experiment has demonstrated that his new idea has at least great practical value for application to every hillside and slope, if not for valley and plain. He claims that it may be worked with wondrous success even on what we call level lands. The central idea of 'The New Agriculture' is the capturing and utilizing by subterranean reservoirs and irrigation, of all the dews, rains and snows for plant growth, and Mr. Cole shows in his side hill experiment that the filtration of the water through the hardest, toughest, most unpromising soil, renders it pliable and most wonderfully fertile and productive."

We must not omit the report made by Mr. James McCann, President, and Mr. George W. Hoffman, ex-President of the Farmer's Club of Elmira. This was presented at a meeting of the Club on July 11th, 1885, and appeared in *The Husbandman* under head of "The New Agriculture:"

"Nearly a year ago the Club resolved to make careful inspection of Hon. A. N. Cole's new system of irrigation, and what has come to be regarded as 'The New Agriculture' but favorable opportunity was not found until Tuesday, July 7th, a day appointed by Mr. Cole, whose invitation to attend for the purpose of examining his work and its results had been received by the Club some days before. Several members who had an earnest desire to accept the invitation found themselves hindered by prior engagements, but President McCann and ex-President Hoffman went as the direct representatives of the Club and were accompanied by several gentlemen more or less nearly related to the institution that gladly accepted them as its representatives. There was much desire on the part of those who attended this meeting to hear the account, and among the number were several that came in after the narration of incidents and observations had been partly made, among them Professor Lazenby, of the Ohio Agricultural College, Hon. J. S. Van Duser, an old-time member of the Club, Thomas Flood, of the city, and G. F. Spinney, of the New York *Times*. Mr. Hoffman's report ran substantially as follows:

"My observations were made mainly with the purpose of attaining clear understanding of the methods by which Mr. Cole had produced what must certainly be regarded as surprising results. But I made no notes, and must therefore rely upon memory in my endeavor to convey to you ideas that impressed me. Notwithstanding what I had read descriptive of the 'The New Agriculture,' and Mr. Cole's account given to the Club some months ago, I had not clear views of his method, and I was therefore quite desirous of making the visit with the purpose of inspecting every part of the work and its results. I found the situation a slope on the eastern face of a ridge, ascending, I judge, four feet in the first hundred. Along this slope trenches were cut on a horizontal line or course, deviating from a straight line when necessary to suit the inequalities of surface, the bottom of the trench having a horizontal run along the face of the slope. The first trench, the pattern after which all other trenches are constructed, is four feet deep and two feet wide, filled with stones to within fifteen inches of the surface, then covered with flat stones and refuse stuff,—grass, weeds, anything to serve as a sort of filter holding the soil placed above to the natural line of the surface, leaving water to drop into the trench and be held for the uses designed. The filling, I was informed, was first by round or shapeless stones gathered from the field, leaving interstices that serve in their aggregate as a receptacle for whatever water may find entrance, principally from rains and melting snows and any springs that may be tapped. It will be seen that the stone filling serves, as the principal purpose, to support the superincumbent earth and the flat stones placed on the top as a kind of cover to prevent the loose soil from dropping into the receptacle below. The horizontal ditches are constructed at suitable distances along the slope, the series intended to hold the surplus of rains so that none flows over the surface. Between these horizontal trenches there are sub-trenches, leading from one of the main excavations to another. These cross-ditches have less depth but otherwise are constructed in the same manner as the main trenches, their purpose to convey surplus of water from an upper to a lower trench, and so equalize the supply. They are filled in the same manner and covered with fifteen inches of earth. The soil is what I may call clay-loam, with stones intermixed, but no appearance of sand, the close, compact subsoil not easily penetrated. I refer to condition before treatment, and of this I had

PLUM, NATURAL SIZE.

fair opportunity to observe in the adjoining land not yet brought under the new system, also in an excavation in progress where workmen had to strike heavy blows with their picks to penetrate the hard clay. The land treated by Mr. Cole was originally part of a considerable tract that was regarded as extremely poor, and my observations led me to conclude that the estimate was just. The most striking effect of the treatment, as it seemed to me, was entire change of character, particularly mechanical condition, due, in large part, no doubt, to the very thorough manipulation, for it is not comprised in the trenching alone. The entire area is dug up to the depth of fifteen inches, and all stones of any considerable size, even down to an inch in diameter, removed, thus changing mechanical conditions to such a degree that one is impressed with the great difference between the land treated and that immediately adjoining. You step upon the trenched land anywhere and you find the soil yields to pressure of the feet, not a spot where it is not soft and yielding; but on the land adjoining it is hard and the foot makes no impression whatever, Another change is in color. That hard, forbidding clay has taken the appearance of muck, or, at least, the color of muck and loam intermixed. Its texture is aptly described by Mr. Cole, who calls it an earth sponge.

"We were called to examine strawberries from plants set, as we were informed, last October, and I am free to say that the plat was a very interesting object inviting study. There was a full crop of most remarkable berries—remarkable in size, color and quality. I cannot undertake to estimate the yield, but it was certainly very large. I called Mr. McCann's attention to one plant of older setting that had ripe berries and others in the various stages of growth, enough, I thought, to fill my hat if they could be picked at one time. One peculiarity of these berries was the absence of what may be termed a core, or hard stem in the middle; they were juicy and tender all the way through. As to the foliage, I can only say that I never saw anything like it. I measured a leaf that was five and one-half inches across, and I plucked a broader one, with Mr. Cole's consent, and brought it home.

"I must say that the changes wrought in the soil and its products constituted a great surprise.

"As to the soil, I could judge by comparison with land that must have been originally of the same character. It now lies hard and compact adjoining the renovated earth, that under Mr. Cole's treatment has certainly become very fertile, whether with manure in abundant supply, or not, I am not prepared to say. The soil under treatment has the appearance of being thoroughly enriched with manure; then there is the water supply for the roots to reach and use, obviating drought apparently; and besides, there is entire freedom from washing. Heavy showers had fallen in the week before our arrival, but there was not the slightest appearance of washing, and Mr. Cole informed us that all danger from washing was obviated; a statement which I can accept as true, for he has provided reservoirs into which all surplus of water must pass, and if there is too much the overflow runs from one to another reservoir. Besides all this the earth worked to fine tilth fifteen inches deep serves as a sponge to take in a great deal of moisture and retain it for the use of plants. Ten days before our visit there was a rainfall of three inches, as reported, and no appearance of washing.

"Of course I can not give you such description as will inform you fully, because one must see what has been done and its results to have complete understanding of the system. I believe there is a great deal of advantage in Mr. Cole's plan, although I may not with my one opportunity for inspection have such full faith as he possesses, for I cannot have such full knowledge as he has obtained in the practical work that has engaged his thought for years. Still, when I see a crop of strawberries much larger than I have ever seen under other conditions, no dead leaves, no runners, growth most luxuriant and long succession in bearing, I must say that results are convincing. There were other proofs about which I am not so well prepared to judge. For instance, an apple tree standing in this improved land was reported worthless, its fruit gnarled and valueless before the land was trenched, now bearing largely and the fruit of fine quality. Of course I cannot say how much difference there is between the tree as it now appears and as it was before the land was improved. I observed, however, a young tree, the trunk five or six inches in diameter perhaps, its growth most vigorous, the limbs smooth as if recently washed with lye, foliage fresh, full and green. But on inquiry I learned that it had only ordinary treatment; the limbs had not been washed, and its vigorous growth was attributed to the system of trenching and irrigating that increased the yield of strawberry plants and the size of fruit, the effect being visible in growth of all kinds. There were no weeds on the ground occupied by strawberries—it was absolutely clean.

"Prof. LAZENBY. There are three or four questions that I would like to ask. What distance apart are the cross ditches?

"G. W. HOFFMAN. I can not say precisely. I asked Mr. Cole, and he told me three or four rods, leaving me to infer that he had exercised no care to place the cross ditches at regular intervals. You will understand that these cross ditches tap the main trench two feet above the bottom, that they are but two feet deep and serve only the purpose of drawing off surplus water, or, in other words, equalizing water in the trenches.

"Prof. LAZENBY. What is done with the subsoil taken from the main trenches? Is it carted away?

"G. W. Hoffman. It is all used on the land, intermixed, I suppose, with the surface soil during the working, as I have said, to the depth of fifteen inches. We saw workmen engaged in excavating a trench, and the compact clay taken from the bottom was distributed over the land to be brought into cultivation. The workmen said that the hard clay would become friable upon exposure, and pointed to places where it had been thrown where it had become soft and yielding. The first working of ground below that trench, we were told, was last May, but the workmen said they would go over it again soon and take out such stones as had been overlooked in the first picking.

"Prof. Lazenby. Still another question—Were those strawberry plants that were put out last October potted previous to placing them in the ground?

"G. W. Hoffman. I do not know that they were; I suppose they were not. They were not as prolific as the older vines.

"President McCann. We were informed that the strawberry leaves kept green all winter, and that the ground was almost free from frost during the coldest weather. Mr. Cole told us that frost rarely penetrated more than an inch or two, while ground not treated was frozen fully three feet deep. Of course, if the soil remains open and there is snow protection strawberry plants may keep fresh and green through winter.

"G. W. Hoffman. There is certainly very great change produced by the new system. How much may be credited to irrigation, how much to very thorough working, and how much to manure, I can not decide. Mr. Cole spoke very highly of forest leaves as a mulch or manure, and, I think, he has made very free use of them. Speaking of leaves, he said: 'They are the very best manure God ever supplied for agricultural use.'

"Now, as to this system of irrigation, there may be a great deal in it I have not seen, although I have seen much to cause surprise. Water flowing out below came clear, no discoloration, and I was told that it was of good drinking quality. Mr. Cole claims that the land will become loose and friable as deep as the trenches. Perhaps this is not overstated. I do not care to speak of claims, nor of opinions not well supported. There is enough in the new system to interest investigators. It is costly. We were informed that the work done by Mr. Cole had cost $500 an acre, but the improvement may be great enough to justify that outlay. I suppose that on an acre set to strawberries there may be 11,000 or 12,000 plants. Now if each one of these produces a quart, the product will give pretty fair interest on $5,000. It must be understood that such remarkable berries as are produced under this system will sell for more than ordinary prices. I want to make another visit later in the season, when we have here the usual summer drought. If I find everything fresh without appearance of drought on Mr. Cole's improved land, I shall regard it as another strong proof of merit in his system."

In conclusion of our introductory or first chapter we beg leave to answer the question asked by Prof. Lazenby by saying that we never pot plants, but grow them, taking pains to catch them in with a trowel, giving them good root. This is done in August and September, and our plants are removed with the trowel quite as often as with the spade, leaving an abundance of earth upon the roots, and they grow right along, though set as late as October, or even November. They grow indeed beneath the snows, and make deep roots in winter.

CHAPTER II.

CIRCULATION OF WATER ON LAND—THE WONDERFUL MESILLA.

To Dr. J. H. Vincent, of Plainfield, N. J., the world is indebted for a system of education reaching the hearthstones and homes of thousands of families all over our goodly land. Chief of these, in form of school or college, is the Chautauqua Literary and Scientific Circle. The organ of this institution is *The Chautauquan*, published at Meadville, Pennsylvania, Theodore L. Flood, D. D., Editor. From the November number of 1883 we copy an article in which, if carefully read and studied, will be found an amount of information which cannot be overestimated in its value to the farming class. Here can be learned the ways of the waters as run by nature's laws, over, through and under the soil. We give this remarkable article in full, for were we to search the literature of the soil to exhaustion, we could not find in so comprehensive and compact a form, a compend upon which to base the text of this volume.

However, before transcribing it, we are equally bound to accord to Mr. Henry Stewart, civil and mining Engineer, member of the Civil Engineers' Club of the North-west and associate Editor of the *American Agriculturist*, the credit of having written, about two years ago, a work on the subject of irrigation from which copious extracts will be found on future pages of our book. Following in the footsteps of progressive experiences beginning, for aught we know, when the deluge in which irrigation was made so general as to drive Noah and his family to seek refuge in the Ark, the author of the volume referred to, "Irrigation for the Farm, Garden and Orchard," confines himself to the subject of applying the waters to the surface of lands, merest mention being made of underground or subterranean methods. Had we the satisfaction of knowing that the farmers and gardeners, the fathers, mothers, sons and daughters of America generally, taking an interest in that most delightful of all pursuits, the one of growing grasses, grains, fruits, flowers, trees and plants in their varied forms, had read Mr. Stewart's book we should omit much of quotation hereinafter made. It is so meritorious a work that we do not hesitate to pronounce it an invaluable adjunct to our own, and would advise every reader of "Our New Agriculture," to couple therewith the study of Mr. Stewart's "Irrigation for the Farm, Garden and Orchard." We now give the article in full from the *Chautauquan*, under the caption of "The Circulation of Water on the Land."

"Although air is continually evaporating water from the surface of the earth, and continually restoring it again by condensation, yet, on the whole and in the course of years, there seems to be no sensible gain or loss of water in our seas, lakes, and rivers; so that the two processes of evaporation and condensation balance each other,

"It is evident, however, that the moisture precipitated at any moment from the air is not at once evaporated again. The disappearance of the water is due in part to evaporation, but only in part. A great deal of it goes out of sight in other ways.

"The rain which falls upon the sea, is the largest part of the whole rainfall of the globe, because the surface of the sea is about three times greater than that of the land. All this rain gradually mingles with the salt water, and can then be no longer recognized. It thus helps to make up for the loss which the sea is always suffering by evaporation, for the sea is the great evaporating surface whence most of the vapor of the atmosphere is derived.

"On the other hand, the total amount of rain which falls upon the land of the globe must be enormous. It has been estimated, for example, that about sixty-eight cubic miles of water annually descend as rain even upon the surface of the British Isles, and there are many much more rainy regions. If you inquire about this rain which falls upon the land, you will find that it does not at once disappear, but begins another kind of circulation. Watch what happens during a shower of rain. If the shower is heavy, you will notice little runs of muddy water coursing down the streets or roads, or flowing out of the ridges of the fields. Follow one of the runs. It leads into some drain or brook, that into some larger stream, the stream into a river; and the river, if you follow it far enough, will bring you to the sea. Now think of all the brooks and rivers of the world, where this kind of transport of water is going on, and you will at once see how vast must be the part of the rain which flows off the land into the ocean.

"But does the whole of the rain flow off at once into the sea in this way? A good deal of the rain which falls upon the land must sink underground and gather there. You may think that surely the water which disappears in that way must be finally withdrawn from the general circulation which we have been tracing. When it sinks below the surface, how can it ever get up to the surface again?

"Yet, if you consider for a little, you will be convinced that whatever becomes of it underneath, it can not be lost. If all the rain which sinks into the ground be forever removed from the surface

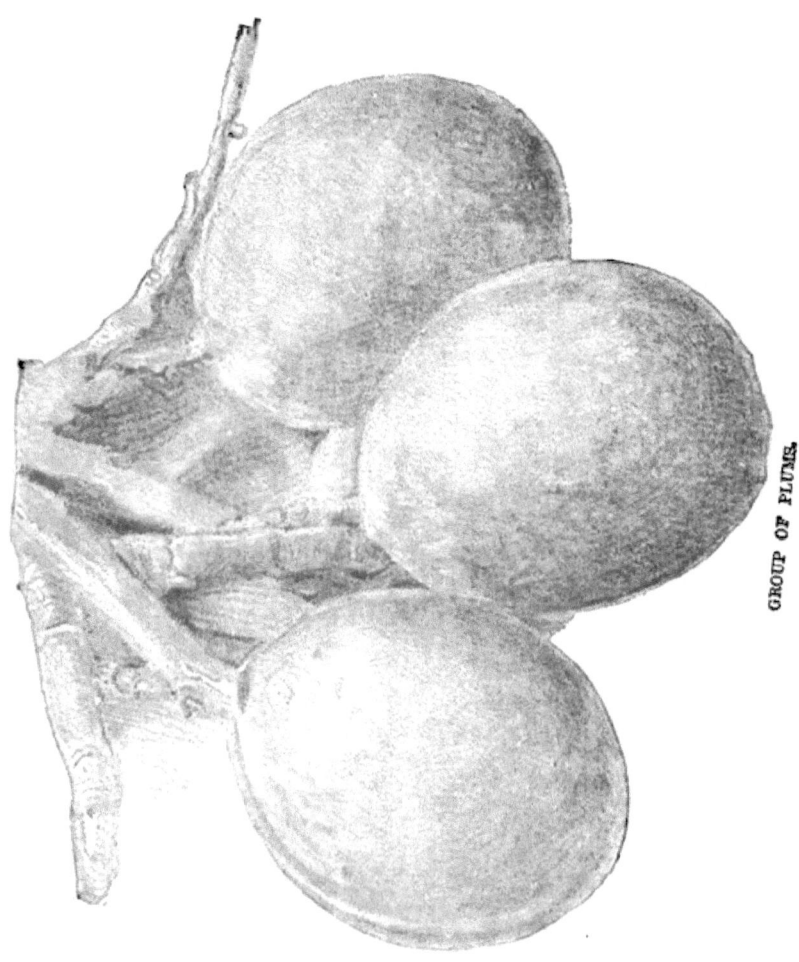
GROUP OF PLUMS.

circulation, you will at once see that the quantity of water upon the earth's surface must be constantly and visibly diminishing. But no such changes, so far as can be seen, are really taking place. In spite of the rain which disappears into the ground, the circulation of water between the air, the land, and the sea continues without perceptible diminution.

"You are driven to conclude, therefore, that there must be some means whereby the water underground is brought back to the surface. This is done by springs, which gush out of the earth, and bring up water to feed the brooks and rivers, whereby it is borne into the sea. Here, then, are two distinct courses which the rainfall takes—one below ground, and one above. It will be most convenient to follow the underground portion first.

"A little attention to the soils and rocks which form the surface of a country is enough to show that they differ greatly from each other in hardness, and in texture or grain. Some are quite loose and porous, others are tough and close-grained. They consequently differ much in the quantity of water they allow to pass through them. A bed of sand, for example, is pervious; that is, will let water sink through it freely, because the little grains of sand lie loosely together, touching each other only at some points so as to leave empty spaces between. The water readily finds its way in among these empty spaces. In fact, the sand bed may become a kind of sponge, quite saturated with the water which has filtered down from the surface. A bed of clay on the other hand, is impervious; it is made up of very small particles fitting closely to each other, and therefore offering resistance to the passage of water, which, unable to sink through it from above on the way down, or from below on the way up to the surface again, is kept in by the clay, and forced to find another line of escape.

"Sandy soils are dry because rain at once sinks through them;

clay soils are wet because they retain the water, and prevent it from freely descending into the earth.

"The rocks beneath besides being in many cases porous in their texture, such as sandstone, are all more or less traversed with cracks; sometimes mere lines, like those of a cracked window-pane, but sometimes wide and open clefts and tunnels. These numerous channels serve as passages for the underground water. Hence, although a rock may be so hard and close-grained that water does not soak through it, yet if that rock is plentifully supplied with these cracks it may allow a large quantity of water to pass through. Limestone, for example, is a very hard rock, through the grains of which water can make but little way; yet it is so full of cracks or "joints," as they are called, and these joints are often so wide, that they give passage to a great deal of water.

"In hilly districts, where the surface of the ground has not been brought under the plow, you will notice that many places are marshy and wet, even when the weather has been long dry. The soil everywhere around has been perhaps baked quite hard by the sun; but these places remain still wet, in spite of the heat. Whence do they get their water? Plainly not directly from the air, since in that case the rest of the ground would also be damp. They get it not from above, but from below. It is oozing out of the ground; and it is this constant outcome of water from below, which keeps the ground wet and marshy. In other places you will observe that the water does not merely soak through the ground, but gives rise to a little run of clear water. If you follow such a run up to its source, you will see that it comes gushing out of the ground as a spring.

"Springs are the natural outlets for the underground waters. But, you ask, why should this water have any outlets, and what makes it rise to the surface? Let us suppose that a flat layer of some impervious rock like clay, underlies another layer of a porous material, like sand. The rain which falls on the surface of the ground, and sinks through the upper bed, will be arrested by the lower one, and made either to gather there, or find its escape along the surface of that lower bed. If a hollow or valley should have its bottom below the level of the line along which the water flows, springs will gush out along the sides of the valley. The line of escape may be either the junction between two different kinds of rock, or some of the numerous joints already referred to. Whatever it be, the water cannot help flowing onward and downward, as long as there is any passage along which it can find its way; and the rocks underneath are so full of cracks, that it has no difficulty in doing so.

"But it must happen that a great deal of the underground water descends far below the level of the valleys, and even below the level of the sea. And yet, though it should descend for several miles, it comes at last to the surface again. To realize clearly how this takes place, let us follow a particular drop of water from the time it sinks into the earth as rain, to the time when, after a long journey up and down in the bowels of the earth, it once more reaches the surface. It soaks through the soil together with other drops, and joins some feeble trickle, or some other ample flow of water, which works its way through crevices and tunnels of the rocks. It sinks in this way to perhaps a depth of several thousand feet until it reaches some strata through which it cannot readily make further way. Unable to work its way downward, the pent-up water must try to find escape in some other direction. By the pressure from above it is driven through other cracks and passages, winding up and down until at last it comes to the surface again. It breaks out there as a gushing spring.

"Rain is water nearly in a state of purity. After journeying up and down underground it comes out again in springs, always more or less mingled with other materials, which it gets from the rocks through which it travels. They are not visible to the eye, for they are held in what is called chemical solution. When you put a few grains of salt or sugar upon a plate, and pour water over them, they are dissolved in the water and disappear. They enter into union with the water. You can not see them, but you can still recognize their presence by the taste which they give to the water which holds them in solution. So water, sinking from the soil downward, dissolves a little of the substance of the subterranean rocks, and carries this dissolved material up to the surface of the ground. One of the important ingredients in the air is carbonic acid gas, and this substance is both abstracted from and supplied to the air by plants and animals. In descending through the atmosphere rain absorbs a little air. As ingredients of the air, a little carbonic acid gas particles of dust and soot, noxious vapors, minute organisms, and other substances floating in the air, are caught up by the descending rain, which in this way washes the air, and tends to keep it much more wholesome than it would otherwise be.

"But rain not merely picks up impurities from the air, it gets a large addition when it reaches the soil.

"Armed with the carbonic acid which it gets from the air, and with the larger quantity which it abstracts from the soil, rainwater is prepared to attack rocks, and to eat into them in a way which pure water could not do.

"Water containing carbonic acid has a remarkable effect on many rocks, even on some of the very hardest. It dissolves more or less of their substance, and removes it. When it falls, for instance, on chalk or limestone, it almost entirely dissolves and carries away the rock in solution, though still remaining clear and limpid. In countries where chalk or limestone is an abundant rock, this action of water is sometimes singularly shown in the way in which the surface of the ground is worn into hollows. In such districts, too, the springs are always hard; that is, they contain much mineral matter in solution, whereas rainwater and springs which contain little impurity are termed soft.

"When a stone building has stood for a few hundred years, the smoothly-dressed face which its walls received from the mason is usually gone. Again, in the burying-ground surrounding a venerable church you see the tombstones more and more mouldered the older they are. This crumbling away of hard stone with the lapse of time is a common familiar fact to you. But have you ever wondered why it should be so? What makes the stone decay, and what purpose is served by the process?

"If it seem strange to you to be told that the surface of the earth is crumbling away, you should take every opportunity of verifying the statement. Examine your own district. You will find proofs that, in spite of their apparent steadfastness, even the hardest stones are really crumbling down. In short, wherever rocks are exposed to the air they are liable to decay. Now let us see how this change is brought about.

"First of all we must return for a moment to the action of carbonic acid, which has been already described. You remember that rainwater abstracts a little carbonic acid from the air, and that, when it sinks under the earth, it is enabled by means of the acid to eat away some parts of the rocks beneath. The same action takes place with the rain, which rests upon or flows over the surface of the ground. The rainwater dissolves out little by little such portions of the rocks as it can remove. In the case of some rocks, such as limestone, the whole or almost the whole, of the substance of the rock is carried away in solution. In other kinds, the portion dissolved is the cementing material whereby the mass of the rock was bound together; so that when it is taken away, the rock crumbles into mere earth or sand, which is readily washed away by the rain. Hence one of the causes of the mouldering of stone is the action of the carbonic acid taken up by the rain.

"In the second place, the oxygen of the portion of air contained in rainwater helps to decompose rocks. When a piece of iron has been exposed for a time to the weather, in a damp climate, it rusts. This rust is a compound substance, formed by the union of oxygen with iron. What happens to an iron railing or a steel knife, happens also, though not so quickly nor so strongly, to many rocks. They, too, rust by absorbing oxygen. A crust of corroded rock forms on their surface, and when it is knocked off by the rain, a fresh layer of rock is reached by the ever-present and active oxygen.

"In the third place the surface of many parts of the world is made to crumble down by means of frost. Sometimes during winter, when the cold gets very keen, pipes full of water burst, and jugs filled with water crack from top to bottom. The reason of this lies in the fact that water expands in freezing. Ice requires more space than the water would if it remained fluid. When ice forms within a confined space, it exerts a great pressure on the sides of the vessel, or cavity, which contains it. If these sides are not strong enough to bear the strain to which they are put, they must yield, and therefore they crack.

"You have learned how easily rain finds its way through soil. Even the hardest rocks are more or less porous, and take in some water. Hence, when winter comes the ground is full of moisture; not in the soil merely, but in the rocks. And so, as frost sets in, this pervading moisture freezes. Now, precisely the same kind of action takes place with each particle of water, as in the case of the water in the burst water-pipe or the cracked jar. It does not matter whether the water is collected into some hole or crevice, or is diffused between the grains of the rocks and the soil. When it freezes it expands, and in so doing tries to push asunder the walls between which it is confined.

"Water freezes not only between the component grains, but in the numerous crevices or joints, as they are called, by which rocks are traversed. You have, perhaps noticed, that on the face of a cliff, or in a quarry, the rock is cut through by lines running more or less in an upright direction, and that by means of these lines the rock is split up by nature, and can be divided by the quarrymen into large four-sided blocks or pillars. These lines, or joints, have been already referred to as passages for water in descending from the surface. You can understand that only a very little water may be admitted at a time into a joint. But by degrees the joint widens a little, and allows more water to enter. Every time the water freezes it tries hard to push asunder the two sides of the joint. After many winters, it is at last able to separate them a little; then more water enters, and more force is exerted in freezing, until at last the block of rock traversed by the joint is completely split up. When this takes place along the face of a cliff, one of the loosened parts may fall and actually roll down to the bottom of the precipice.

"In addition to carbonic acid, oxygen and frost, there are still other influences at work by which the surface of the earth is made to crumble. For example, when, during the day, rocks are highly heated by strong sunshine, and then during night are rapidly cooled by radiation, the alternate expansion and contraction caused by the extremes of temperature loosen the particles of the stone, causing them to crumble away, or even making successive crusts of the stone fall off.

"Again, rocks which are at one time well soaked with rain, and at another time are liable to be dried by the sun's rays and by wind, are apt to crumble away. If then it be true, as it is, that a general wasting of the surface of the land goes on, you may naturally ask why this should be. Out of the crumbled stones all soil is made, and on the formation and renewal of the soil we depend for our daily food.

"Take up a handful of soil from any field or garden, and look at it attentively. What is it made of? You see little pieces of crumbling stone, particles of sand and clay, perhaps a few vegetable fibers; and the whole soil has a dark color from the decayed remains of plants and animals diffused through it. Now let us try to learn how these different materials have been brought together.

"Every drop of rain which falls upon the land helps to alter the surface. You have followed the chemical action of rain when it dissolves parts of rocks. It is by the constant repetition of the process, drop after drop, and shower after shower, for years together, that the rocks become so wasted and worn. But the rain has also a mechanical action.

"Watch what happens when the first pattering drops of a shower begin to fall upon a smooth surface of sand, such as that of a beach. Each drop makes a little dent or impression. It thus forces aside the grains of sand. On sloping ground, where the drops can run together and flow downward, they are able to push or carry the particles of sand or clay along. This is called a mechanical action; while the actual solution of the particles, as you would dissolve sugar or salt, a chemical action. Each drop of rain may act in either or both of these ways.

"Now you will readily see how it is that rain does so much in the destruction of rocks. It not only dissolves out some parts of them, and leaves a crumbling crust on the surface, but it washes away this crust, and thereby exposes a fresh surface to decay. There is in this way a continual pushing along of powdered stone over the earth's surface. Part of this material accumulates in hollows, and on sloping or level ground; part is swept into the rivers and carried away into the sea. As the mouldering of the surface of the land is always going on, there is a constant formation of soil. Indeed, if this were not the case, if after a layer of soil had been formed upon the ground, it were to remain there unmoved and unrenewed, the plants would by degrees take out of it all the earthy materials they could, and leave it in a barren or exhausted state. But some of it is being slowly carried away by rain, fresh particles from mouldering rocks are being washed over it by the same agent, while the rock or subsoil underneath is all the while decaying into soil. The loose stones, too, are continually crumbling down and making new earth. And thus, day by day, the soil is slowly renewed.

"Plants, also, help to form and renew the soil. They send their roots among the grains and joints of the stones, and loosen them. Their decaying fibers supply most of the carbonic acid by which these stones are attacked, and furnish also most of the organic matter in the soil. Even the common worms, which you see when you dig up a spadeful of earth, are of great service in mixing the soil and bringing what lies underneath up to the surface.

"One part of the rain sinks under the ground, and you have traced its progress there until it comes to the surface again. You have now to trace, in a similar way, the other portion of the rainfall which flows along the surface in brooks and rivers.

"You cannot readily meet with a better illustration of this subject than that which is furnished by a gently sloping road during a heavy shower of rain. Let us suppose that you know such a road, and that just as the rain is beginning you take up your station at some part where the road has a well-marked descent. At first you notice that each of the large heavy drops of rain makes in the dust, or sand, one of the little dints or rain-prints already described. As the shower gets heavier these rain-prints are effaced, and the road soon streams with water. Now mark in what manner the water moves.

"Looking at the road more narrowly, you remark that it is full of little roughnesses—at one place a long rut, at another a projecting stone, with many more inequalities which your eye could not easily detect when the road was dry, but which the water at once discloses. Every little dimple and projection affects the flow of the water. You see how the raindrops gather together into slender streamlets of running water which course along the hollows, and how the jutting stones and pieces of earth seem to turn these streamlets now to one side, and again to another.

"Toward the top of the slope only feeble runnels of water are to be seen, but further down they become fewer in number and at the same time, larger in size. They unite as they descend, and the larger and swifter streamlets at the foot of the descent are thus made up of a great many smaller ones from the higher parts of the slope.

"Why does the water run down the sloping road? Why do rivers flow? Why should they always move constantly in the same direction? They do so for the same reason that a stone falls to the ground when it drops out of your hand; because they are under the sway of that attraction toward the center of the earth, to which, as you know, the name of gravity is given. Every drop of rain falls to the earth because it is drawn downward by the force of attraction. When it reaches the ground it is still, as much as ever, under the same influence, and it flows downward in the readiest channel it can find. Its fall from the clouds to the earth is direct and rapid, its descent from the mountains to the sea as part of a stream is often long and slow; but the cause of the movement is the same in either case. The winding to and fro of streams, the rush of rapids, the roar of cataracts, the noiseless flow of the deep sullen currents, are all proofs how paramount is the sway of the law of gravity over the waters of the globe.

"Drawn down in this way by the action of gravity, all that portion of the rain which does not sink into the earth must at once begin to move downward along the nearest slopes, and continue flowing until it can get no farther. On the surface of the land there are hollows, called lakes, which arrest part of the flowing water just as there are hollows on the road which serve to collect some of the rain. But in most cases they let the water run out at the lower end as fast as it runs in at the upper, and therefore do not serve as permanent resting-places for the water. The streams which issue from lakes go on as before, working their way to the sea-shore. So that the course of all streams is a downward one, and the sea is a great reservoir into which the water of the land is continually pouring.

"The brooks and rivers of a country are thus the natural drain, by which the surplus rainfall, not required by the soil, or by springs, is led back again into the sea. When we consider the great amount of rain, and the enormous number of brooks in the higher part of the country, it seems, at first, hardly possible for all these streams to reach the sea without overflowing the lower grounds. But this does not take place, for when two streams unite in one, they do not require a channel twice as broad as either of their single water courses. On the contrary, such an union gives rise to a stream which is not so broad as either of the two from which it flows. But it becomes swifter and deeper.

"Let us return to the illustrations of the roadway and rain. Starting from the foot of the slope, you found the streamlets of rain getting smaller and smaller, and when you came to the top there were none at all. If, however, you were to descend the road on the other side of the ridge, you would probably meet with other streamlets coursing down hill in the opposite direction. At the summit the rain seems to divide, part flowing off to one side, and part to the other.

"In the same way, were you to ascend some river from the sea, you would watch it becoming narrower as you traced it inland, and branching more and more into tributary streams, and these again subdividing into almost endless little brooks. But take any of the branches which unite to form the main stream, and trace it upward. You come in the end to the beginning of a little brook, and going a little farther, you reach the summit, down the other side of which all the streams are flowing to the opposite quarter. The line which separates two sets of streams in this way is called the watershed. In England, for example, one series of rivers flows into the Atlantic, another into the North Sea. If you trace upon a map a line separating all the upper streams of one side from those of the other, that line will mark the water shed of the country. But there is one important point where the illustration of the road in rain quite fails. It is only when rain is falling, or immediately after a heavy shower, that the rills are seen upon the road. When the rain ceases the water begins to dry up, till in a short time, the road becomes once more firm and dusty. But the brooks and rivers do not cease to flow when the rain ceases to fall. In the heat of summer, when perhaps there has been no rain for many days together, the rivers still roll on, smaller usually than they were in winter, but still with ample flow. What keeps them full? If you remember what you have already been told about underground water, you will answer that rivers are fed by springs as well as by rains.

"Though the weather may be rainless, the springs continue to give out their supplies of water, and these keep the rivers going. But if great drought comes, many of the springs, particularly the shallow ones, cease to flow, and the rivers fed by them shrink up or get dry altogether. The great rivers of the globe, such as the Mississippi, drain such vast territories, that any mere local rain or drought makes no sensible difference in their mass of water.

"In some parts of the world, however, the rivers are larger in summer and autumn than they are in winter and spring. The Rhine, for instance, begins to rise as the heat of summer increases, and to fall as the cold of winter comes on. This happens because the river has its source among snowy mountains. Snow melts rapidly in summer, and the water which streams from it finds its way into the brooks and rivers, which are thereby greatly swollen. In winter, on the other hand, the snow remains unmelted; the moisture which falls from the air upon the mountains is chiefly snow; and the cold is such as to freeze the brooks. Hence the supplies of water at the source of these rivers are, in winter, greatly diminished, and the rivers themselves become proportionately smaller."

In conclusion of this chapter, and by way of complete demonstration of the wonderful effects of subsurface irrigation, we quote from an article telling a story which, read by the average farmer and gardener, cannot fail to prove convincing. These surely will be glad to know that the way has been found to escape the calamities to which producers have been hitherto subjected on account of frosts, floods and droughts. Nor will it become necessary to argue the case in the newspapers and publish books to convince them that to adopt our system is the way and the only way open to reliance upon a full and perfect crop year in and year out.

Having in previous chapter made mention of the subterranean river in lower California, where, in the midst of the desert is found a valley of perpetual green abounding in rarest productions of the fruits of the earth, we proceed to quote from the article referred to, as it appeared in *Harper's Monthly* for April, under head of "Along the Rio Grande."

"It was the wonderful fertility of the far-famed Mesilla which led to its purchase from Mexico by the United States, under the Gadsden treaty, moving the boundary about thirty miles southward and making American citizens of the Mesilleros. La Mesilla is a charming looking place with luxuriant gardens and noble trees densely shading its streets. The United States land office for the southern part of New Mexico is here, and the great excess in the number of paid up mining claims over those of the northern district at Santa Fe, speaks well for the prosperity of the mining interest of the section.

"Contemplating the uncultivated soil, one wonders where the Mesilla Valley got its fame for fertility, since it apparently consists of barren sand, tufted with rank weeds. But an abundance of sunshine and water, works wonders here, as is testified by the rich tilled fields, and the many beautiful orchards and vineyards. The profits of agriculture here are great. One of the leading citizens of Mesilla, is said to have an annual income of something like ten thousand dollars from eighteen acres of vineyard and orchard. Several hundred acres of prairie land would hardly accomplish so much. The mildness of the climate is shown by the existence of a beautiful large fig tree in the *patio* of one of the Mesilla houses. Considerable Mesilla wine is now taken east by the railway, and it is averred that in the hands of New York dealers, the Mesilla label is not infrequently replaced by the legend "Fine Old Sherry"'

"The onion is a famous product of the Mesilla Valley; it grows to an enormous size—larger than I have ever seen or heard of elsewhere. Onions seven or eight inches in diameter are not uncommon.

"The *Acequias madres*, the "mother canals" of the irrigating system, broad and shaded by fine trees, are a beautiful feature of the scenery. Their water is of a tawny orange, and flows as rapidly as the river. It is genially warm; delightful for bathing, despite the abundant earthy matter held in suspension. The fear has been expressed that it would be hardly possible to irrigate the Mesilla Valley much more extensively than at present, as the water supply is scanty, and in some seasons the river runs dry altogether; but it is likely that a system of wells would make the water supply ample enough for all demands.

"In Syria extensive vineyards are irrigated from large wells dug for the purpose, and some day it may be found profitable to apply the same idea to the Mesilla Valley. The water of the river underlies the whole valley bottom. A few feet below the ground at any place water is always found in abundance. This accounts for the magnificent trees in La Mesilla. Their roots strike down into the ground water, so that in the driest of weather and fiercest of heats, they are never athirst, but always proudly lift up their crowns of deep emerald. Fruit trees, after a good start, never require irrigation. They grow very large here, and in the enormous peach trees one would hardly recognize the short lived tree of the North."

CHAPTER III.

DESCRIPTION OF THE NEW SYSTEM—"HOME ON THE HILLSIDE"—THE HOT WATER METHOD.

Those of our readers who have followed us through the introductory chapter and especially in that section of it where the methods of "The New Agriculture" have been described by visiting farmers and agricultural editors, have not failed to get a succint idea of the new system, hence it is unnecessary for us to give in this chapter more than a simple resumè of the methods adopted by us at our "Home on the Hillside."

The processes of "The New Agriculture" are so simple and plain that the average intelligence can not only understand and apply it, but having so conformed soils as to set the system in operation, he may go to sleep and leave it to run itself, which it will do, year in and year out, winter and summer alike, and so perfect will be found its work at all times as to result in the utmost possibilities of production.

To conform soils under our system, the ordinary laborer has only to move along the hillside with plow, pick and spade, sinking trenches three, four or five feet wide, and as many feet deep; of sufficient depth, at least, to drop the waters below the frost lines, guided by no level other than the water moving along the bottom of the trench. Then cast in round stones to the depth of from eighteen inches to two feet, and shingle perfectly with flat ones when obtainable, and flat tile or timber where stones are not accessible, and in the absence of round stone, making use of tile so conformed as to secure reservoirs. Then rake out the fine stone from excavations for use in the construction of overflow trenches, in which, if stone is not procurable, use tile, perforated or those leaking at joints, or making use, if disposed, of other suitable material.

On reaching level or bottom lands during construction, the overflow trenches should be so constructed as to secure a continued flow through them from each successive reservoir trench.

Let no reader doubt that, in regions where rains and dews descend and snows fall, the waters, always in motion so that stagnation in no case occurs, will not only find their way into the trenches filtered and filtering as they flow, but will emerge in form of springs or enter streams at their bottoms, with soils of the surface remaining unwashed and steadily fertilized by the flow of waters through them. When the waters come to the cold clay and clod of the subsoil the latter will be aerated, warmed, loosened and rendered soft, porous and productive to the depth of the deepest trenching, and every acre thus treated will be increased in value and that permanently to a degree vastly lucrative.

Let us suppose that a farmer has a hillside and that he has adopted our system, in which case he goes to work as follows:

A ditch is opened on a water-level along the side hill or slope, say a yard wide and from three to five feet deep. At the bottom of this ditch is loosely placed cobble and blocky stones for a foot or two, then flat stones are laid over these, then a quantity of smaller stones; cover these over with weeds, briars, bramble, fine brush, straw, cornstalks or any available material, to prevent the fine earth from falling among and filling the crevices between the stones. A heavy coating of manure may follow and then the excavated soil is to be spread over it, grading a terrace if desired. Whatever course the trench may take, the surface of the hard-pan at the lower side of the ditch or trench must never vary from a water-level. A series of such ditches, one above the other, are dug a rod or so apart and similarly filled, over as large a surface as is to be improved, each forming an elongated reservoir which will be filled by the water courses cut off, or by the melting snows and early rains; and, if the subsoil is firm clay or hard-pan, it will be retained and as the surface soil dries it will be absorbed by capillary action and brought within reach of the roots of vegetation. See diagrams on opposite page.

In regions where the conditions are favorable, suffice it to say that land fitted as above described, will with wonderful celerity and great economy produce most surprising results.

If the reader will take the above brief description of our methods and consider it carefully in connection with the cuts illustrating our system, he will find no difficulty in understanding the principles of its construction. A few points only remain to be stated to make it perfectly plain:

In soils where fine stone can be raked out, it should be done for the purpose of constructing the connecting overflow trenches. These overflow trenches should be in the subsoil, and filled with fine stone to a depth of a foot, at least, and shingled with flat ones in the same manner as the reservoir trenches. All shingling should be of sufficient depth to escape the plow or the deepest spading.

The construction of overflow trenches, bearing the waters from the reservoir at base of slope, will need to be as perfectly done as possible. The finer the stone below the shingling, and the more

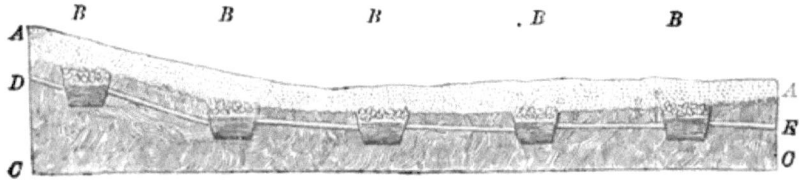

A A. Surface soil.
B. Trenches.
C. Subsoil.
D. Overflow trenches.
E. Outlet or drainage trench.

Patented July 22d, 1884.

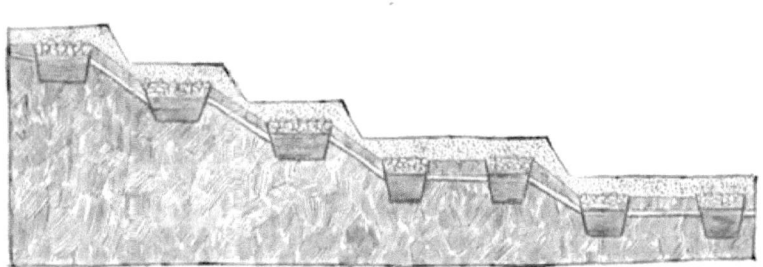

DIAGRAMS OF NEW SYSTEM.

perfect the shingling, the more complete will filtration be found, the more crystal the waters as they emerge into the stream and the more complete will be the work of leaving solids behind as food for plants. The head of the overflow trenches at base of slope should be at least twelve or eighteen inches above the bottom of the reservoirs. In most cases, when the flat or bottom land of the valley is reached, the construction of overflow trenches should have an oblique direction towards the stream, or lowest point aimed at, in order to secure sufficient fall to keep the waters freely moving. Two or three inches of fall to the rod will be ample and where this is not obtainable, less will suffice.

On the west bank of the Genesee, at a point about twenty miles from its source, is found our "Home on the Hillside," with its model five acres, where the author of this volume is engaged in demonstrating what may be done by conformation of soils and conservation of the waters. Nothing has been, or will be, left undone to make our model so far perfect as to develope the entire possibilities of production, hence calculations of cost, based upon our own experiment, will be found greatly at fault. An equal area put under conditions ensuring an average yield annually of from three to five fold of that hitherto realized under former systems, would likely be cultivated by parties gardening for profit; in this case the expense would be only from one-fourth to one-half of the amount laid out on our model.

The location of our home, could not well be improved, looking out as it does toward the East at the sun in its rising. A town of about four thousand population lies in the valley below, through which runs the far famed Genesee River for a distance of about forty miles above the Portage. In confluence with the river at this point several tributaries unite, forming dells of rare beauty and attraction. All about the town rise up lofty hills on which are seen comfortable dwellings with cultivated fields surrounding. A few only of the summits remain forest crowned. No town within our knowledge of like population, boasts a larger number of elegant dwellings. In looking out from our observatory, the view is one far reaching, both up and down the valley, and it is seldom surpassed.

Not completely is our home a model, nor do we propose to present it as such, and yet, having planted here the garden whose green in the season has no parallel, altitude and latitude considered outside of isothermal influences, we assume that the accompanying engraving of it will be of interest to our readers. Were the hillside of gentler slope, the effect would, in the eyes of some people, be a more pleasing one, and yet, such has been the effect of spade, pick, hoe and rake, as to make gradation so uniform and gentle in decline, as to produce a most pleasing effect. So tall and symmetric are the trees crowning the summit, and so lustrous the green of the garden, whether in bud, blossom or fruitage, such is the scene presented as to delight all who visit us. Here in midsummer when the season proves one of ordinary fruition, will doubtless be discovered a greater wealth of production than on any equal space, not under glass, in America.

Above and to the west of the house, covering an area of less than two acres, trenching, fitting and planting to trees, bushes and vines is complete. The trenches above do not quite flank the rear of the lawn to the east of the house, embracing about the sixteenth of an acre. The lawn is planted with trees, chiefly the sugar maple, grown to impressive proportions. The surface of the lawn is one of the gentlest incline and were it not for injury to roots of the trees trenching would be forthwith pushed to the south and east, as already done to the north and west of the house, so that the green of the grass at all seasons of the year might evidence the magic inspiration coming of conserved waters at spring water temperature. Let nobody conclude however that we propose to let our lawn remain in its present condition. Despite possible damage to our trees from cutting off a portion of their roots, we propose to trench this lawn and make connection with the network of trenches and drains to the north and west of the house, thus surrounding the earth with hidden waters, warmer in winter and cooler in summer than the atmosphere.

The question will doubtless be asked, can homes everywhere be thus environed? Our answer is, yes, beyond doubt, especially those located on hill and mountain sides, slopes and inclines; and that too, regardless of subsoil. That this can be more economically and readily done where firm clay or hard-pan subsoils are found, than on those where these conditions do not exist, is true, but we repeat our declaration that it can be done on other lands by the use of substitutes, doing no more than facing the bottom of the trench to the depth of two or three inches with clay, cement or flat tile, thus permitting the trench to fill with water during rains. If reserve is an object it can be accomplished by facing the lower wall of the trench with like material within two feet of the surface, and by arranging an inclined plane of kindred material, thus holding the waters in uniform currents of overflow from trench to trench. Whatever the character of subsoil existing in lawns, dooryards, gardens and grounds surrounding the dwelling, systems of reservoirs, planes and inclines can be so arranged as to prove automatic, and the waters kept moving in continuous flow, feeding and watering grasses, plants and trees at deepest root, always in abundance, and never in surfeit.

Certain gross misrepresentations have been made and reports set in circulation that we had made use of springs or other natural and artificial sources of supply to secure results reached under our system of subsurface, subterranean or underground irrigation. All of these have not enough of foundation to be dignified by contradiction. There is not one man in America of ordinary intelligence who is not capable of understanding, after reading the preceding pages of this volume, that a system which gathers in all of the waters coming of rains, dews and melting snows, begetting perpetual irrigation during every month in the year, needs no artificial sources of supply, and we will not insult our readers by entering upon a discussion of so absurd a supposition that after saving all waters falling from the clouds upon a given watershed, more is needed for the growth of plants. Under old methods and conditions fully nine-tenths of the water of rains, and nearly all waters of melting snows, have been wasted in floods, hurried off by the insensate use of tile, or absurd systems of drainage; and when it comes to snow waters, these nearly all reach the streams along frozen grounds and are lost. Under our system all are saved, such portions used as needed, and the remainder passes off in purity to streams in the valleys.

Up to this point, discussion has been confined to the uses and influences of the waters as they fall from the clouds, and find their way into trenches at spring water temperature.

Now, however, we will treat of that feature of our system wherein a steady stream of cold water, drawn from a trench or reservoir above, is passed through a coiled pipe or boiler, and then emerging, is dropped into the trench, the stones heated and by surface protection. the winter months are, to a great extent, made those of production. Let the following serve as an illustration.

"A curious experiment has lately been made at Acqui, Italy, by the proprietor of some baths there. The gentleman has at his disposal an inexhaustible supply of hot water from a natural spring, the temperature being 167 degrees Fahrenheit. The surplus not required for the baths has been diverted so as to flow through pipes to a garden on the outskirts of the town. Here the warm liquid flows beneath a number of forcing frames containing melons, tomatoes, asparagus and other garden produce. The result is that a supply of these delicacies is ready for market at a very early period of the year, when, therefore, they fetch high prices."

The significant feature of this method is the fact that evaporation of the waters at this high temperature is graduated and kept up night and day by heating of the stones in trenches constructed on substantially the same principles as those sunk under our system, hence the results realized. The great drawback hitherto, to the adoption of methods in this country, akin to those of Europe, viz. that of bottom heat, has been the difficulty and expense attending keeping up fires night and day, securing the uniformity of temperature required for success. The case in which the barber in Italy quoted above makes use of the waters of hot springs to turn winter into summer, is by no means an isolated one, since in many cases throughout Europe, this is being done, and with gratifying success. The finest of pineapples and other tropical fruits are grown in England by bottom heat. There is no good reason why the expensive, and in many instances unsatisfactory methods of glass and green-house should not give way in our own country, and that Europe should have the monopoly of growing the hardier varieties of vegetables and fruits in midwinter, when by surface protection of cambric dipped in oil, and by the addition of glass the fruits of the tropics may be readily grown in this country.

Not unlikely our book may fall into the hands of readers unaware of the fact, that natural gas as fuel is being used in thousands of households in certain sections of our country. The cold winter through which we have passed has not been nearly so rigorous with ourself and neighbors on account of this wonderful agency. Not only Wellsville but Friendship, Cuba, Bolivar, Richburg, Allentown, Genesee and others of our Allegany county towns in the state of New York are being supplied with it, but Pittsburgh and numberless other cities and towns of Pennsylvania, Ohio and West Virginia, have been, and are being, made recipients of its blessings. No fuel compares with it, nor is any provision of the Creator of greater benificence. Discovery of its existence, to a greater or less extent, is being made in all parts of our country, and so soon as the inhabitants of colder and more inhospitable regions find out that they have only to dip down with the drill, and bring up from the cold clods of earth a fire which burns night and day, comforting many of the inhabitants of earth, there will be less digging for gold, and more for golden opportunities.

Let nobody wait, however, for gas developement in order to apply our system as a substitute for the greenhouse. Coal and wood are abundant in most portions of our country, and these can be used for heating water with which to warm the stone in the trenches.

CHAPTER IV.

PRACTICAL RESULTS OF THE NEW SYSTEM.

Mr. Stewart in his practical work prints the following notes on the growth of crops more especially those of grasses:

"What are the ultimate possibilities of growth in any crop is unknown, but it would seem as though they depended greatly upon the supply of water absorbed, sufficient nutriment, of course, being provided. Rye grass upon irrigated fields, richly fertilized, has grown at the rate of one inch per day, and repeated cuttings have been made at intervals of fourteen days, during a season of months. Crops of grass on irrigated fields of a total weight of more than eighty tons per acre have been reported by trustworthy English farmers. Irrigated grass fields in Italy support easily two head of fattening cattle per acre, every year, and have long done so. In hundreds of localities in European countries are irrigated meadows, which have borne grass without any sign of deterioration within the memory of the inhabitants, or the knowledge of readers of local histories, although the crop has been cut and removed every year during this indefinite period. Whether or not these immense crops could be further increased by more skillful management is not neccessary to inquire. These products are so far beyond the dreams of an American farmer, that they may be well considered fabulous. But there is no reason to doubt the facts. On the contrary, they should be used as a stimulus for us to adopt, wherever practicable, the methods by which these crops are produced."

The methods above referred to are those of surface irrigation, which, when compared with those of subsurface are, in results, as fractions to units.

We have as before stated, grown three perfect crops of timothy in a season under conditions not nearly as favorable as those secured under our system as at present existing. This can be done not only by the farmers of New Jersey, Pennsylvania, Ohio, Maryland, the Virginias and Carolinas, but in New York, New England and the more northern states generally, and quite as well in regions still farther north, where snows fall deeply, and remain upon the ground during the entire winter. These are facts, and as such should result in insuring adoption of our system wherever American thrift, intelligence and enterprise prompt to action.

In the cultivation of the vine, there opens a field so wide as to make its growth a source of wealth not easy to estimate. Along mountains and hillsides, where grapes are grown, there is almost invariably found pools of water, deep hidden in chambers of stone.

From these the waters should be dropped, below the frost line, where, warm in winter and cool in summer, moving from trench to trench, the health of the vine, hence its wealth of production, is promoted. Mr. Stewart opens the ninth chapter of his book as follows:

"It is doubtful whether there is an orchard or vineyard in the United States, except in California, Utah or Colorado, subjected to systematic irrigation. At the same time it is doubtful if there is any country in the world in which irrigation could be more profitably applied to fruit culture than here. The experience of orchardists proves that drouth is accompanied by destructive attacks of insects. How far these depredations might be prevented by irrigation cannot be predicated, but it is beyond doubt that the vigor of growth that would result from a sufficient supply of moisture to the roots would greatly mitigate the effects of these attacks. The apple trees which never have an off year are those grown near bodies of water. A California vineyardest who irrigated his vines, immediately raised his product to eight tons of grapes per acre, and greatly improved the quality. The newly planted orange groves of Florida are frequently destroyed by drouth, and methods of irrigation are eagerly sought to render their culture more safe and certain. But if it were necessary to enforce the advantages of the irrigation of orchards, abundant evidence could be gathered in the south of France, Italy and other countries of southern Europe, where the olive, orange, lime, almond, fig, apple and other orchard trees, as well as the vineyards, are systematically brought under irrigation. As to the vine, it is a question, so far, which has not been thoroughly investigated, whether or not irrigation might be made the means of vanquishing the destructive phylloxera."

Possibly our readers may weary with our much quoting from a single author. If other testimony than that of Mr. Stewart were required, the field from which to gather is a wide one, but Mr. Stewart has gleaned facts from all sources and we find in his book the history of the experience of individuals and peoples covering many centuries, hence the invaluable character of his conclusions.

Among American authors, few, if any, are more popular than E. P. Roe, who writes with a versatility of information and talent upon almost every subject, and upon none with greater acceptance than upon those of agriculture and horticulture. Before us, as we write, lies an elegant volume entitled "Success with Small Fruits." This is an expensive work, and all the more a pity since a book containing so much of knowledge and combining so many attractions, should be within reach of all classes. Mr. Roe's book is one of three hundred pages, six only of which are devoted to the subject of irrigation, and brief as is the chapter treating of it, the author makes apology for devoting even so much space to consideration of a matter ere long to be recognized as one of paramount importance. At the opening of the chapter on irrigation he says:

"This is a topic on which a book might be written."

If Mr. Roe will look into our system, perhaps he will be inclined to write another book. Sincerely do we wish he would do so, since there is a recognized charm about his writings making the dullest subject one of interest.

"The question, as we shall consider it," says Mr. Roe, "is a practical one. In California and other sections, the land *must* be irrigated; here, and where the rainfall is more equally distributed throughout the year, we can water if we find the practice remunerative."

Mr. Roe quotes Mr. W. D. Philbrick as saying:

"The amount of water required will depend largely on the rainfall, velocity of the wind, atmospheric humidity, soil, etc. A loose, sandy soil will require much more water than a retentive clay. In general, however, it may be assumed that, in the warm growing months of May, June, July, August and September, most vegetation requires an inch in depth over the entire surface of the land every five days. This is, of course, only an average. This quantity, estimated as needed by our gardens, would be equivalent to six inches per month of rainfall. If we compare this amount with the actual rainfall, we shall arrive at an idea of what is to be supplied artificially. The rainfall at Boston for the past six years 1873-1878, for the five growing months named, varied from a maximum of $10\frac{1}{2}$ inches in August, 1872, to a minimum of 0.65 inch, in June, 1873. During these six years there was not a single season when we did not suffer more or less from drought during some portion of the summer. Twenty-one of the thirty months in question had less rainfall than six inches per month, and the average of those twenty-one months was about 3.02 inches per month, or only about half of what was needed. Some of the protracted seasons of drought were almost entirely rainless for six weeks, during which the weather was excessively hot and windy, and vegetation suffered extremely in consequence."

But why multiply witnesses touching the necessity of saving, instead of wasting the waters? In our colder climates of the North, the waters of rains, dews and melting snows should all be halted, housed, husbanded and held back so far as may be, getting all possible advantages from them. As we write, there comes to hand a letter from Hon. John Swinburne of Albany, N. Y., which will find its place on the pages of our book, alongside of another from the pen of Hon. C. R. Early of Pennsylvania. Both these gentlemen are representative men, eminent in public, private and professional life. Both agree that the future of the waters is the one of the world. The one would gather them in, purify and use them to make an end of fungus, deadliest enemy of vegetable and animal life; the other shows how this can be done, and vividly portrays the advantages to come of the achievement.

Let no reader conclude that, from the frequent mention made along these pages of firm subsoils, that these are the only ones where our system will apply. It can be applied on all soils to great advantage. Two out of three among correspondents writing us have asked whether our system can be made to apply to level lands. Our answer is, it will apply everywhere. The relative advantages of its application are those of economy, and the lands to which it is most readily adapted will be found the most profitable.

Not in the North, where demonstration of its great utility has been first made, is it to perform its greatest wonders, but in the South, the land of cotton and corn, will be seen its greatest triumphs. Corn as a crop and for ensilage, and sorghum and beets for sugar, can be grown to an extent and with a measure of success hitherto unparalleled. Orange groves can be doubled and trebled in yield, and not merely the English grasses, but all varieties of fruits can be grown to a degree of perfection hitherto unattained. And then too, the orchard.

Who shall estimate the wealth to come to North, South, East and West from a system causing trees to grow, though planted amid droughts? Nor only so, but a system under which the old fruit tree becomes young and vigorous, making new roots, dropping its scurvy bark, its parasitic mosses, and doubling, trebling, quadrupling, and not unfrequently quintupling its yield of fruit.

How about potatoes? Let us answer this question by stating results as regards a single row planted in the spring of 1883. We had planted on lands near by for an early crop, when nearly a fortnight later finding space for a row immediately below one of our completed trenches, devoted it to the Early Rose variety. The first planted potatoes appeared above the ground five or six days in advance of this test row. By the first of June, the latter showed much larger and finer growth of vines than the former, and the potatoes of both matured about the same time, the 25th of July. All were perfectly ripe, the earliest planted, however, were dwarfed by blight, and more or less eaten by wire worms, their average size being about that of a hen's egg. The vines of our test row lived their full life, and died a natural death, showing a crop of marvelous size, beauty and perfection. Suffice it to say that not a single potatoe was found rotted in our test row, nor was there the mark of the "tooth" of a wire worm found. The potatoes averaged the size of a goose egg, and a few specimens were as fine as the very finest we have ever seen. The yield from this one row was nearly or quite three times as much as from any grown that season on our own grounds or on those of our neighbors of equal area. In nearly or quite every hill outside of the test row, was found from one to three or four rotten potatoes, and these, as usual, were the largest ones.

Why this very great difference? nearly or quite every reader will naturally enquire. Here is our answer: No uncomposted manure was mixed with the soil, and consequently no seeds of fungus were sown. On lands above the trench, manures were spread between rows of raspberries, while still farther up our manures had been corded for composting. The snows of winter and rains of early spring had sent their waters in flow adown the incline, and when our first trench was reached, these were dropped into its depths and the trench filling and overflowing, the waters passed through the sponge of our single row, feeding the tubers with "broth, soup or porridge," and hence there was perfection in growth and fruition. This accounts for the fact, attested by Dr. C. R. Earley, in his chapter on fungi, that nowhere on our grounds is that deadly enemy of vegetable and animal life to be found.

Perhaps the point has not yet been reached to propound the question ere long to be everywhere asked: Will it pay to drink water and grow fruits uncontaminated with stagnation and other sources of infection and contagion? In other words will it pay to grow fruits and vegetables to sell, which, when eaten by yourself and family, are liable to engender disease and produce death, when by the simplest of means, through adoption of methods discovered and fully demonstrated, those of far greater perfection and with larger profits, can be grown free from infection, and perfect in all ways.

How about vineyards? Can more grapes be grown under systems of subsurface irrigation than by ordinary methods in countries of rainfall? That surface irrigation has been found a necessity in arid regions, is well understood; and there also, have the finest grapes of the world been grown. Up to this time, however, no vineyard, so far as we are aware, has been planted under circumstances, and cultivated under conditions conforming to the utmost developement of the vine and product. The terrace is constructed and when the rainfall is abundant the waters, descending the incline, are checked in degree by the level of the terrace, but when this becomes dry and baked the water of brief showers moves off in rapid flow, and, if the shower is a hard one, the terraces in groups come little short of presenting an appearance of successive cascades. In rainless regions, where provision is made for irrigation by mechanical means, and in those of an abundant rainfall, so numerous have been the cases of failure to realize a crop as to have had a discouraging effect.

In no regard has Mr. Stewart's book more profoundly impressed us, than his frank confession throughout the work of the impossibility of so applying water to the surface, as to insure profitable results. Nothing could be more convincing of the superiority of our system than this confession.

After devoting a large amount of space to prove that winter irrigation of meadows and pastures has proven not only successful but profitable in climates of Southern Europe, and demonstrating the fact that in all portions of our own country where the ground freezes only to the depth of a few inches or not at all, irrigation in the winter months would have wonderful effect in continuing the growth of grasses at their roots, Mr. Stewart hands over to the hopeless desolation of winter the regions in which dwell millions of our most intelligent, enterprising and thrifty people by saying that "in the Northern States and Canada, winter irrigation is impracticable."

In turn, we do not hesitate to declare, that if a series of trenches along inclines was constructed from three to five feet deep, at any and all points in the States of New England, New York, New Jersey, Delaware, Pennsylvania, Ohio, Michigan, Illinois, Iowa, Wisconsin, Minnesota and throughout the Canadas, Nova Scotia and New Brunswick, dropping the waters of autumn rains so deeply down as to hold them during winter at spring water temperature, they would be found to melt the snows at bottom and hold the trenches nearly or quite full of pure spring water during every day of winter.

In no particular do we propose to leave demonstration incomplete. The following article from the Chicago *Journal* tells the story:

"When the hair on the heads of the young and rising generation shall have been whitened with age; when their descendants of the, second generation shall be toddling around their great arm-chairs or begging to be taken on their knees and told some stories of the, to them, mysterious past, the grandparents will, no doubt, on many such occasions recall the winter from which we are just emerging, but which has clung so tenaciously to the lap of spring, and which still seems so unwilling to leave us, and speak of it as the terrible winter of 1884-85, when the thermometer for fully one-third of the whole season remained below zero, and when, during the entire months of January and February, the mercury rose to the freezing points or above on only fifteen occasions; when snow-storms were of almost daily occurrence, and when the regular spring-time of the year had run considerable of its course before the great mountains of snow, which had almost hidden the earth, had disappeared from view. It can not even now be gainsaid that the past winter was a pretty tart one. Setting in as it did about the middle of December, it has continued with the full force of its rigor till the end of March, and its whole course has been marked with the fewness and long distance apart of its intervals of mildness. Its record for severity cannot be surpassed by that of many seasons in the present century.

"The coldest day of the year, taking it all together, was February 10, when the thermometer stood at 16 degrees below zero for almost the entire twenty-four hours, though at other times it sank for a short time as low as 30 degrees below.

"Below will be found a record of the dates on which the thermometer was below zero between 8 a. m. and 1 p. m.:

"December 17, 2 degrees; 18, 12; 19, 7. January 2, 4 degrees; 13, 5; 14, 10; 19, 17; 20, 8; 21, 6; 22, 16; 26, 7; 28, 15. February 10, 16 degrees; 11, 13; 12, 3; 13, 10; 15, 10; 16, 13; 17, 7; 18, 2; 19, 1; 20, 9. March 20, 2 degrees.

"The dates in January and February when the thermometer rose above freezing were:

"January 5, 6, 7, 8, 9, 10, 31, and February 2, 3, 4, 24, 25, 26, 27 and 28."

Unless other winters of greater severity remain in store for the present and future generations, we have no hesitation in declaring that our system is good for irrigation from December to April of any year likely to come while there remains alive a single child now born, and we believe at any parallel of latitude between Mason and Dixon's lines, and Hudson's Bay. Certain is it, that Southern Alaska can safely count on having been released from subjection to the dominions of the Frost King, since it has been discovered that this hitherto little understood portion of our country possesses a climate producing crops vastly superior to those of the more northerly countries of Europe and Asia, and that grasses can be made to greenly grow all winter beneath the snows of this most inhospitable of our territorial possessions.

The article quoted from the *Chicago Journal*, will, we are sure, convince every reader that the past one has been a winter throughout the North and East, justifying us in saying that so far as Allegany County, N. Y. goes, that farmers using our system may defy the Frost King.

It is three years since the Hon. Warner Miller, so ably and eminently representing New York in the United States Senate, remarked:

"If you can realize the results claimed under your system, Mr. Cole, and I incline to believe it, then our State is capable of maintaining a population within its limits of an hundred millions, supported in comfort, from agriculture and horticulture alone,"

If this is possible in the State of New York, we ask our readers to read the following copied from *The Northwest*, of March, 1884, and estimate what our system would do when applied to the most inhospitable, and hitherto deemed, from an agricultural point of view, hopeless region embraced within the boundaries of the American Union:

"Alaska is a broad peninsula situated at the northwestern extremity of the continent, washed on the south by the mild waters of the Pacific and on the north by those of the frozen Arctic. Upon its frozen and deeply indented shore line, towering and rugged headlands enclose quiet and picturesque coves and harbors, within many of which the united naval fleets of the world might float, secure from the storm-tossed billows of the encompassing oceans. Extending back from its coast is a broad zone of fertile lands, characterized by wide-reaching plateaus and magnificent valleys, richly clothed with native grasses, and watered by deep-flowing, majestic rivers.

"Within its interior the Rocky Mountains attain their greatest altitude north of Colorado, Mt. St. Elias, near its southern boundary, towering to the height of 17,000 feet. The mountain regions are distinguished by immense forests of pine, fir, cedar and hemlock, sometimes extending in an unbroken growth for many miles upon the lower portions of the range, and broad low-lying basins, (ancient lake beds), shadowed by naked, rocky cones and snow-clad peaks. The climate of Alaska is not so intemperate as its northerly situation would indicate, the Kurho-Siva or Japanese current, an ocean stratum of heated waters, flowing from the South Pacific, exerting upon it a climatic influence, analogous to that of the Gulf Stream upon the British Isles. Moist, warm winds blow across the Alaskan sea-coast regions, and the Aleutian Islands, situated near, in the Behring Strait, lending to them a delightful summer climate, and rendering them fruitful in the extreme. The fiftieth isothermal, which leaves the eastern coast of Asia near Pekin, strikes the continent of North America near the 50th parallel of north latitude, then trending rapidly to the south, passes near the region of the great lakes, and leaves the eastern coast of the continent, near the city of New York,

"Thus we find the climate of the lower regions of Alaska very similar to that of Wisconsin, Michigan, and the New England States. The records of the Signal Office established at Sitka for five years, show the mean temperature of the year to be the same in Alaska as in Minnesota and Wisconsin, and the productive power of the soil is certainly equal to that of any portion of the northeastern part of the United States."

That this is no picture of fancy, we have occasion to know as a few hours further sail of the steamer which, a year ago, bore us to Victoria the capital of British Columbia, situated on Van Couver's Island and lying in the same latitude as northern New

Foundland, would have borne us into Alaskan waters. Here at Victoria fruit trees had dropped their blossoms, and apples, pears, plums and other fruits were developing. No spot of earth was greener nor one blander and more summer like in atmosphere. Keeping no diary, as nearly as we can fix the date from memory, we left Victoria the last of April, and reaching our Allegany County home on the sixth of May, found our family and neighbors just beginning work in their gardens. While our own little plat was a fortnight ahead, even this was fully three weeks behind what we had found the gardens of Victoria to be ten days before. The calculation is therefore a safe one, that the average March of Victoria is the May of Allegany, and that the springs of Southern Alaska average as early as those of Western New York.

On the 13th day of April, within a week after the departure of the snows, the soil of our garden being soft and porous, its surface having been warmed by the sun, we began garden making by putting in peas, onions, lettuce, beets, etc. Though all around and about, the earth was frozen to the depth of from two to four feet, upon that portion fitted under our system not a particle of frost was discernable. Having begun garden making on the 13th of April, a week later visiting New York and casting our eye out of the car window going and coming, in no spot did we see the commencement of seeding. In fact, we were assured by Alfred Henderson, son of Mr. Peter Henderson, seedsman, of New York City, that work in the open grounds of New Jersey had not begun, and that in shaded spots all over the northern portions of that State, frost remained in the ground.

Such, nevertheless, was the condition of the soil in our garden at the period of first seeding, that germination immediately followed, and our peas, sowed on the 13th, were out of the ground on the morning of April 28th; onions were sprouted, and other seeding had resulted in germination. Our rhubarb, or pie plant which had shot up into the snows before their departure was large enough for use, and the promise, made to the Jerseymen present on the occasion of our address before the Farmers' Club of the American Institute had been made good, the present season finding us ahead of New Jersey in planting our garden. When we say that Allegany County, N. Y., is usually a fortnight, and not infrequently three weeks behind New Jersey in the opening of the spring, it will not be questioned that water in trenches at spring water temperature produces wonderful results. That the producing season will be lengthened from forty to sixty days on lands fitted under our system, may be therefore set down as a fact.

The virtues of "The New Agriculture," was most severely tested on the morning of April 28th. The wind was in the southeast, and the mercury at 10 A. M., stood at 50° above zero, and reached 65° at noon; the day was one of spring balm. It began raining about 3 P. M., the wind south, and the shower was one more of May than April. Shifting suddenly into the north, Boreas put on the lion in earnest and a violent snow storm ensued. The night was one of severe coldness and when we awoke at 4 A. M. on the 29th, we made up our mind that if there was virtue in cold water, this was the time to test it. Repairing to our garden, the frigid condition of the ground all around, outside of our two acres, was about as hopeless as in dead of winter. Beneath our feet, however, the soil yielded, and upon making examination we found no frost. The "noses" of our peas, sticking out of the ground, had a look much more nearly blue than green. Only the day before, meeting friends in Elmira, we had boasted of our pie plant, challenging comparison with any grown in open grounds either in New York or New Jersey. These, however, to our discomfiture, next morning were found

STRAWBERRY BOUQUET.

frozen to the consistency of an icicle, breaking like glass on bending. Observing however that the ground was not frozen, we concluded that the root was not killed, and, by way of experiment, we subjected the frozen stalks and leaves to a cold bath. Repairing to a pile of forest leaves, we bore several bushels to our plants, and covering them deeply, poured upon each hill, four pails of water, drawn from the hydrant near by. The saturation was complete. The sun rose coldly, and shone out in a frigid way all day, and yet, had we not protected them by the wetted leaves from the effects of its rays, there would probably have been an end of pies for a fortnight thereafter. Once or twice during the day, we ventured to take a look at our frozen plants, and each time had more and more hope of saving them. Removing the leaves on the 30th, we found our pie plant uninjured. Precisely one year before, we ate rhubarb pie at a hotel in Victoria, British Columbia, grown in the open ground, beneath the balmy breezes of the Japan current. A little upwards of a week later we reached our Allegany home, but ate no rhubarb pie till after the middle of May.

Our five hills of rhubarb or pie plant were four years ago (1881) transplanted, and in resetting, were planted along the line of one of our leads or overflow trenches. Not till last fall, however, were they so connected with the reservoirs, as to keep a steady stream of water running beneath them, and since September last, the flow has not ceased. And so it was, that on the departure of the snows about April 10th, our pie plant had shot up into its snowy covering, getting the start of any in our State by a week or or ten days. It is not only in this, but in numberless other ways we have demonstrated the fact that a stream of spring water running beneath will give inspiration to the growth of plants in winter It is in this regard that our system differs, and in fact is distinct from all methods hitherto proposed and in some instances put in operation through means of perforated tile, begetting what has been denominated sub-irrigation.

Tile has been laid to considerable extent in California, Nevada, Colorado and New Mexico, and the resulting irrigation has been found phenomenally successful, leaving that of the surface methods completely in the shade. There has been a patent allowed on the tile, but not upon the system, yet the ordinary drain tile answers every purpose, leaking sufficiently at joints to diffuse the waters. To lay a network of this tiling at sufficient depth to escape the effects of frost in winter, more especially in regions where the freezing reaches a depth of several feet would be a most expensive and unpromising undertaking at best, and when to the great expense of this mode of preparing lands to receive the water, is added that of making provision for water supply dependent upon springs, streams, artesian wells, windmills, current wheels, and the thousand and one other devices necessary to such a system, not one man in a thousand can be found to give the thing a moment's attention especially if he farms in rainfall sections. We desire here to give the wonderful history of the old apple tree that stood and now stands renewed in life upon our hillside. This tree, the only fruit bearing one on our original plot, was upwards of thirty years old, and before trenching began was so unthrifty, covered with moss and in all ways so unpromising as to incline us to cut it down as a cumberer of the ground. Nor was the tree alone undesirable. The fruit, a golden russet, grew no larger than what is known as the lady apple, nor nearly as large as we have for the last two years grown strawberries in certain instances. The fruit was so tough as to be left in the cellar until all other apples were gone, and not unfrequently thrown away in the end. Not to exceed a bushel and a half had been gathered from the tree in any one season previous to 1883. In the month of October, 1882, a deep and model trench was sunk immediately above this June russet apple tree. The spring succeeding, the wealth of blossoms on this tree was surprising. The blossoms were of a size attracting attention of even the children, being nearly twice the size of the ordinary apple blossom. The fruit developed rapidly, and by the first of August the apples had reached a growth larger than at any time before when the fruit was harvested. Such was the weight of the fruit as to necessitate the propping of nearly every limb. When the apples ripened, complete transformation was discovered. Little, if any russet coating was to be seen, the fruit having dropped its color and coating, and some of the better specimens would have passed for greenings.

When Mr J. F. Langworthy visited us, we presented him with specimens of plums of the size of an ordinary hen's egg, picked in his presence from a tree which, before our system was adopted, had never given them larger than a small pullet's egg. Specimens of these plums were also sent the same year, (1883), to Hon. R. E. Fenton, ex-Governor of our State, and exhibited in New York to Hon H. J. Jewett, President of the N. Y. Lake Erie and Western Railroad Company, and to Alfred Henderson, son of Mr. Peter Henderson, and were pronounced by all to be the finest specimens they had ever seen.

While Deacon B. F. Langworthy was looking over our grounds, we plucked heads of timothy of second cutting, eight inches in length, fully seeded, and subsequently cut others, a third crop averaging six inches. As near as we can now recollect, the first of these cuttings was about the middle of June, the second the last of July, and the third about the middle of September. In the first cutting the heads averaged nine inches, and in some instances reached ten, and in one, at least, eleven inches in length and of most surprising weight. Specimens of the Kittatinny blackberry were also presented to Deacon Langworthy of such marvellous size and beauty, as to excite wonder. We also showed Mr. Langworthy four rows of the Philadelphia red raspberry, in which the bushes were so heavily laden as to make it impossible to stake them sufficiently to prevent the bushes from being prostrated by the wind. As near as we could calculate, the yield would have equalled five hundred bushels to the acre. This, however, is mere guess work, since to pick the berries as fast as they ripened was impossible, and more than half of the crop perished.

That hillside lands having clay or hard-pan subsoils valued at fifty dollars per acre, and scarcely paying at that, will have their soils deepened and rendered correspondingly productive, and at an expense not exceeding fifty dollars per acre in trenching, become permanently improved, paying splendidly on from two to five hundred dollars per acre, we have no doubt. Although different views may exist as to the increase in value of farm lands by adoption of our system, when it comes to the matter of gardening and fruit farming, our own experience is conclusive.

It has only been four years since the first stroke of work was done on our model five acres. We have now about a quarter of an acre of strawberries, plants three years old in August of the present year (1885); not far from an eighth of an acre two years old; another eighth, eighteen months old, and a quarter of an acre will be a year old the last of September, 1885. Our first quarter of an acre, three years old the present season, will be found only good for the half of a full crop, from the fact of having imperfectly done our work at the beginning. Our currants, raspberries and blackberries are just fairly coming into bearing, also our quince, pear and plum trees. When all are in full bearing, (which we cannot count upon short of five years yet), to put the income from our five acres at five hundred dollars and upward per acre is perfectly safe, marketing what fresh fruits and vegetables we can at or near home, and evaporating and preserving the remainder. It is equally as safe to calculate that, were a like five acres situated near any of our great northern cities, the profits would be correspondingly increased. It is no uncommon thing, as we note by the newspapers, for strawberries to sell in the New York markets during the holidays, which can be done under our hot water system, for several dollars per quart. One acre of strawberries, at the rate we have grown them, would bring a sum we leave to our readers to calculate.

Before us lies a letter received some time since from Mr. F. G. Jones, of Keuka, Putnam County, Florida, who writes:

"If there could be found out a way to retain the water here for future use to all plants, Florida would become one of the richest fruit growing states in the Union. We have a rain nearly every day all summer, but it sinks below the surface almost immediately, and as the soil is sandy will not retain moisture like northern soils. I want to set some strawberries this fall. They do well here, and are gathered from January to July, and bring from twenty-five cents to one dollar and twenty-five per quart."

From all portions of the South as well as from States like New Jersey, Delaware, Maryland, Missouri, and notably from states and territories embraced in what has been denominated the Great American desert, letters have been coming for months, asking all sorts of questions touching our system. The burden of these is always the same, "the droughts, the droughts, how shall we escape the droughts." But for the ordinary farmer, one who is cultivating from fifty to an hundred, and thus on to thousands of acres, the question again is, will it pay? To this we answer, if any farmer doubts it, let him make experiment on a single acre of meadow land. Let him try an acre of potatoes, beans, peas or corn on trenched lands, and compare results, year in and year out, and if it is not found to pay immeasurably better than any farming he has ever done, our five acres are growing lies.

Not a day passes but there comes to our place the farmer, the fruit grower, the gardener, the greenhouse man, each in turn looking over our grounds, and are filled with amazement at results, and yet they still ask, will it pay? All agree that it will pay *us* to expend five hundred dollars in fitting an acre to perfection, and yet question whether it will pay other people, costing no more than from fifty to an hundred dollars an acre according to conditions of soil and original lay of the land. We went to work four years ago on one of the most unpromising spots possible to imagine, and did next to nothing with the team, plow, scraper, or anything else indeed but the pick, spade, hoe, potatoe digger and rake; our hard clay and gravelly hillside abounded in stone, with little of surface soil, and we were at an expense twice as great as that to which the horticulturist would be ordinarily subjected.

When it comes to agriculture, the same amount of work could be done in most instances at from a third to a fifth of the cost, fitting lands in a way to grow two, and probably three perfect crops of grass of from three to four tons each annually to the acre, from five hundred to a thousand bushels of potatoes; from an hundred to an hundred and twenty-five bushels of oats; an hundred bushels of shelled corn on an average, and other crops in proportion.

A perpetual green of grasses can be realized in regions of the North where snows fall deeply, and lie on the ground during the winter, since the water in the trenches constructed under our system are dropped beneath the frost line, and such is their effect upon soils, as to prevent freezing, and the hardier varieties of plants are made to grow greenly beneath the snows. The regions in which this can be most economically, readily and perfectly done, are those of hills, valleys and undulations having firm clay or hardpan subsoils, where an abundance of stone, round flat and fine, are found in the soil. This class of lands are, in fact, the most valuable for purposes of agriculture and horticulture in the world. Upon and along them, will, within a few years, be found the loveliest houses, the richest peoples, the finest farms, and gardens, and in their neighborhood and vicinity, the grandest cities of the world.

We have found no difficulty in convincing every man who has examined our methods of gathering in and flowing on and out of the waters, that these can be controlled in subsurface flow, yet there are few who have yet realized the fact, that, when there is a general adoption of our system the springs of the primeval forest are to not only reappear, but that hundreds and thousands of others will develope, forming rivulets and rivers, growing lakes, the latter alive with trout and other varieties of fish, presenting a scene akin to transformation of the earth's surface.

Fearing that we might occasionally mislead people to adopt our system if we published estimates based on the actual cost of trenching to us, we have counted as an investment all moneys expended, not merely for fitting of lands, but for manuring, making, harvesting and marketing products, as well for plants and trees set upon our grounds. Three acres of our plat, or thereabout, are being prepared for strawberries. On this portion all stone, big and little are taken out and placed in trenches. To do this, as it appears to us, pays better than to leave the work imperfectly done. Few people, perhaps, will be found to agree with us, however favorably lands to be fitted may be located in proximity to profitable markets.

We note that the question has been asked:

Do our trenches ensure this marvellous growth and perfection of fruitage, or is it not rather the fifteen inches of fine tilth upon a hard pan subsoil which we have formed, that holds the rainfall producing the extraordinary results as exhibited on our hillside?

That fifteen inches of fine tilth will produce a marvel of growth we well know, for years ago we tried the experiment by dipping as deep down as possible with spade and fork, securing fifteen, possibly twenty inches of fine tilth, growing the Triomphe de Gaud strawberry and other fruits to marvellous size, beauty and perfection. It cost us more to secure that fifteen or twenty inches of fine tilth on *one-sixteenth of an acre,* than it is now costing to secure an equally productive one five feet deep on a *full acre* by trenching.

A few weeks since, among invitations received, asking us to discourse on systems of irrigation and drainage came one from Mr. Newel Cheney, Secretary of the Western New York Agricultural and Horticultural Association, for an address at Cuba, Allegany County, during the annual meeting of said association on the 11th and 12th of June. Coupled with this invitation came also a pamphlet containing report of proceedings and addresses at last year's annual meeting of the association held at Randolph, Cattaraugus County, March 13th, and 14th, 1884. Among addresses on that occasion none was read with greater relish than that by Prof J. T. Edwards, D. D., of Randolph, N. Y., on the Conewango Valley, which consists of a dead level of "about forty thousand acres of oozy, unproductive swamp lands." In the opening of his address, Professor Edwards asks how these swamps can be converted into beautiful farms, waving with timothy and clover. From first to last, the Doctor gives us a compend of good things. That Doctor Edwards gave becoming directions as regarded straightening the bed of the creek, and so deepening it at one point as to set the waters in rapid flow along the valley beyond, is evident. So far as the Doctor goes, he makes no mistake, but stops short at the very spot where he should have gone ahead. Pointing to Europe, he says:

"Holland, for instance, is one of the most prosperous countries in the world, a land where banks never fail, where pauperism is unknown, and bankruptcy unheard of. It is held against the hourly protest of the sea. The houses rest upon piles driven into the soft earth, yet its drainage is so perfect, that its productiveness is wonderful. The dykes cost more than sixty millions of dollars. It is the best example of plucky farming on the planet."

To cover the case the Doctor should have added that, Hollanders have found out the way and put it in practice, how to drain and irrigate, irrigate and drain, not starving by fits and stuffing by starts, but feeding and watering the vegetable kingdom, always abundantly and never in surfeit, never attempting to grow crops in the way some people do pigs, with a streak of fat and a streak of lean, but so arranging their dykes and ditches as to keep the waters always moving through their soils.

Let us suggest that should the State of New York continue in its determination not to extend aid to undertakings such as reclaiming the swamp lands of the Conewango Valley, and a stock company will organize and purchase the entire forty thousand acres and do precisely what Doctor Edwards proposes, not stopping there, but sinking trenches and cross drains for overflow in a way to do what the Hollanders have done, and though it were to become necessary to manufacture tile, conforming them to the work in hand, thirty dollars an acre at least can be made, or in the aggregate, one million, two hundred thousand dollars.

The Doctor tells us that three kinds of land are found in the swamps, one composed of deep muck, another of fine silt reaching an unknown depth, and a third composed of a mixture of the two.

There are probably very few stones, if any, found in the soil, and recourse to tile would become necessary. The rains, dews and waters coming of melting snows should be dropped at the least four feet deep, with overflow drains or tile and cappings about eighteen inches beneath the surface. Such perforation of the tile should be made as to most evenly and generally diffuse the waters, and if all is done in a common sense way, so pure will these be found, so uniform the temperature, that dwellers in the Conewango Valley will every year see a green Christmas, and instead of growing frogs, toads, lizards and the like, will be able to bring out lakes crystal clear all along the track of their waters, alive with bass, perch and pickerel, and not unlikely the mountain trout of California, or possibly those of the brooks of Allegany, Catteraugus and Chautauqua, of an half century ago.

CHAPTER V.

THE INFLUENCE OF THE NEW AGRICULTURE UPON THE HEALTH OF MAN AND DOMESTIC ANIMALS—COMMUNICATION FROM THE HON. JOHN SWINBURNE—THE BANE OF FUNGUS, BY PROF. C. R. EARLEY.

It is the last of June (1885) and all over the country come reports of drought, nor any wonder. The tile manufacturers and their patrons must by some means find out that this hurrying off and drying up of the waters, is a most serious matter, and one which, persevered in, will result in disasters greater, first or last, than has been as yet realized in any civilized land. New York City, with her vast population is fearful of an impending water famine. Doctors Edson and Taylor recommend the purchase of a tract of land half a mile wide on each bank of the Croton River to provide against contamination of its waters. This recommendation should be heeded. The entire water shed of the Croton ought to be purchased, trenched and planted to trees; made a park, and filled with babbling brooks and crystal lakes and stocked with trout. That the water supply would, under such conditions, be found at all times abundant for a city as large as London, New York and Paris we are inclined to believe.

This brings us to the introduction of a witness whose reputation is such as to need no endorsement from us, standing as he does in the front rank of American physicians and surgeons—the Hon. John Swinburne, late Mayor of the city of Albany, at one time Health Officer of the Port of New York, and now Member of Congress elect from the Albany district.

ALBANY, May 7th, 1885.

Hon. A. N. Cole:

DEAR SIR:—After quite thorough examination and consideration of your invention, or system styled by you "The New Agriculture," I have become deeply interested in the matter, and beg leave by letter to express to you the impressions I have formed in reference to it.

Careful thought about the system impels me to the conclusion that as a plan for the storage and preservation of waters for irrigation and purposes of general use, it demands and merits far more attention at the hands of farmers, gardeners and the public generally than has as yet been given to it.

In a country like ours—in the eastern, southern and central portions fast filling up with large cities and villages and thickly populated neighborhoods—the question of the most available means of obtaining a proper and sufficient supply of water for mechanical manufacturing and household purposes, and for protection against fires is calling to its consideration the earnest attention and careful study of many of our ablest scientists and most practical thinkers; while to agriculturists, manufacturers and mill owners generally, in these sections, the very perceptible decrease in the volume of our rivers, creeks and other irrigating streams, upon the sufficiency of the supply of water from which they have been compelled heretofore (some in part and others wholly), to depend for success in their various avocations, has been to many of them the cause of great diminution of business and business profits, and to others a subject of deepest anxiety. The reduction of our forests, it is said, (and very properly too), has resulted in a consequent reduction of our rivers and streams, which were once freely navigable from their mouths nearly to their sources, until they are now only kept open for commerce in many parts by the application of great labor and large expenditures of money almost continually. And as have failed these larger streams, so have also their smaller tributaries (from which they all in fact derive their supplies), become lessened in volume, until at length farms which were once properly and abundantly watered are now comparatively without supply, and streams which once furnished sufficient water-power for the running of mills and factories, now scarcely afford power sufficient to propel the churns of the farmers occupying their banks. The depreciation in the value of lands in many parts of the country for agricultural purposes, and in the supply of crops therefrom, and from the same cause, has become equally perceptible. Yet, the supply of water from the clouds—from rains and snows—has not, so far as we know, in any way decreased;—but the forests are not here to husband them, and these waters are permitted to soak into the ground, or run to waste from the surface almost as soon as they strike the earth.

The problem heretofore has been how best to secure and husband these supplies, by artificial means, so as to most effectually preserve them for the vast demands of our wonderfully increasing population, for family and business purposes, and especially so as to make them more useful in the cultivation of the soil.

Many able and ingenious thinking men have for a long time given this question their attention; and many plans have been suggested—some of greater and some of less merit—but all accompanied with an apparent intricacy of detail and weight of expense in their application, which has prevented the general or considerable adoption of either.

But you, Mr. Cole, seem at last to have discovered a scheme, plain and practical in itself, and evidently of but moderate expense in its adaptation to the uses and necessities of a very large proportion of the people who are now suffering severely from the evils to which I have above called attention. You style your system "The New Agriculture," and from its probable effect upon agricultural districts in which it may be hereafter adopted, as indicated by the experiments you have already made, the name would not seem to be in any way misapplied. If the results of its use in general should be an increase in crops and vegetation, to but half the extent foreshadowed or promised by those experiments, (and I can see no sufficient reason why your claims in this respect may not be fully verified by practical application of your plan) you have developed and now offer to the country and the race a new system for husbanding the falling waters and a new plan for their use which will not only establish a new era in agriculture, but which may be so used as to afford the needed supply of good, healthful and pure water for the other ordinary uses of life to very many sections of the earth, where the inhabitants are now suffering disadvantages and deprivations from its want.

Your plan or invention is exceedingly simple in detail, and the greatest wonder to any one who shall see or read of it will be, that it had not been thought of, developed and adopted long before. It bears the impress of reason and sound sense upon its first presentation to the mind and more mature reflection upon its merits only results in more strongly developing these characteristics in it. The scientist and the plow-boy alike can each with equal promptness and facility perceive its scheme and merits at a glance, and the person who proposes to use it on his farm or garden, or in connection with his shop, dwelling-house, mill or factory will not require the assistance of the scientific and mathematical knowledge of the civil engineer or architect to enable him to

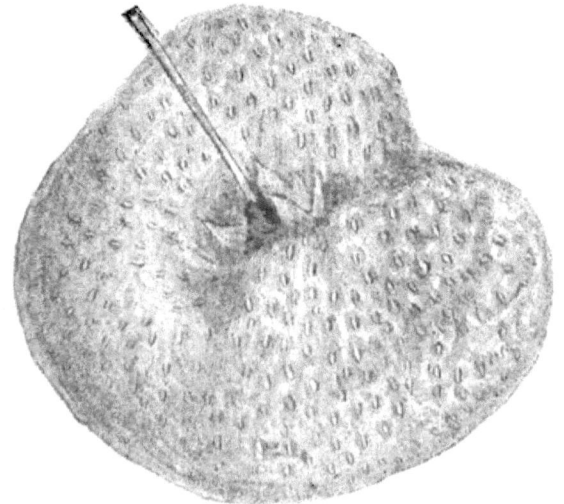

STRAWBERRY, NATURAL SIZE.

put it in successful operation, the brain of an astute accountant to estimate its cost, or the eye or mind of the learned student of nature to discover its results. Combining in itself a plan for the accomplishment of these objects highly essential to the comfort, convenience and business interests of the people,—storage of water, irrigation and drainage,—it will be seen at once by even the ordinary mind upon most casual inspection, to be practicable and feasible for either purpose, and it must be equally evident that great advantages must accrue to the user of the system either for agricultural purposes, the storage of water for other general uses, or as a means of drainage simply.

Scarcely a township exists in our country, in which there are not many farms upon which your admirable system could be applied to great advantage and profit. Large portions of territory in agricultural districts are now entirely useless, or at least comparatively unproductive, by reason of insufficient irrigation; and these through the appliance of your "New Agriculture," could be made vastly more productive; while the present productive portions would be increased in productive power through the same instrumentality. To the grape and other fruit growers, it seems to me, it affords especially inducements for use, which will speedily bring it into imperative demand with the large majority of this important business class. Through it thousands of agriculturists in every state may easily and with little expense make their barren wastes to smile with productiveness, and the better portions of their farms to double in value by reason of increase in crops.

But the advantages to be derived from the use of your plan in the storage of water for other than agricultural purposes are equally apparent, and must eventually bring it into active demand and use in localities where the supply of water is now insufficient for the requirements of cities and villages; and by its application many such corporations will be enabled to furnish their citizens with good, cool and pure water, in sufficient quantities, and at far less expense than they can by any other plan or system now known. Of course, whether it can be so utilized as to furnish very large cities with sufficient supply is a problem hereafter to be demonstrated; but in our own state, (and without doubt in every other state), there are hundreds of smaller cities and thickly populated villages and hamlets, whose inhabitants are now suffering great inconvenience, and incurring risks of sickness and death from malarial and epidemic diseases, from insufficient supplies of healthful and pure waters—whose surroundings are such that, by the reasonable application of your simple system for collection and storage of water they could each, at much less cost than in any other way, be furnished with a permanent and sufficient quantity of the best of water for all the purposes for which it may be required by them. Then too, the hills or mountains surrounding or adjoining these places,—often now utterly unproductive, and sometimes even unsightly in appearance,—can by this same plan be transformed into productive and ornate terraced gardens, far excelling in products and profit the ordinary agricultural lands of the neighborhood and rivaling in beauty the most famous of the ornamental gardens of the old world,—presenting at all times "a thing of beauty" to the eye, season by season affording more profitable remuneration to their owners from the crops and fruits and vegetables which shall spring from and adorn their slopes; and at the same time and always affording to the inhabitants of the populous places beneath their shades a bountiful supply of Heaven's best and only beverage for man.

I am confident that your system will grow in popularity with its use; and eventually a grateful people, thankful for the blessings your invention has brought to their hands, will rank you as a benefactor of the human race, who has not only succeeded in making two blades of grass grow where one was wont to appear; but who has also taught them by simple method, and at cheapest cost, the way to secure for themselves a sufficiency of one of the most important of God's gifts to man, and beast, and nature.

This letter requires no answer—it is written to testify my appreciation of the merits of the invention of an old friend, and he is at liberty to use it as he may deem proper.

With sentiments of respect I am, as ever, yours truly,

JOHN SWINBURNE.

The case of water poisoning, at Plymouth, Pennsylvania, should operate as a warning that all over our land water works have been and are being constructed, in the sources and supplies of which are found the germs of disease and death. Whatever the source of water supply filtration is imperatively necessary, except where springs or spring brooks discharge their waters so directly into reservoirs as to prevent infection, pollution, or even the existence of roil. Can waters admixing with those of the surface be rendered pure and healthful, is the paramount question. This brings us to the introduction of an article by Professor De Smedt, District Chemist, of Washington, D. C., as published under date of June 26th, the subject being the water of the Potomac river.

" Is perfect filtration and aeration possible in a volume of water sufficient to supply large cities? This is a question for the consideration of engineering science; the chemist can determine only the results of the scheme should it prove to be practical.

" Water, in the order of its purity, may be divided into three classes: First, rain water, which is the most impure; second, river water; and third, spring and deep well water, which are the purest. The purity of the spring water is owing to the fact that it has been filtered and aerated through sandy soil, which is indisputably the most perfect purifier of water containing organic impurities; this is demonstrated by natural facts. Spring water, generally so pure and limpid, proceeds from surface waters polluted with vegetable and animal impurities, but becomes purified during its passage through the earth. This evidence furnished by springs, is confirmed by practical results of the irrigation of sewerage instituted in England and France. Finally, the proof is made conclusive by analysis and scientific experiments that perfect artificial filtration can produce water almost as pure as spring water.

"Water, more or less polluted, having passed through a deep filter composed of sand, containing a small percentage of argillous matter, the insoluble particles are stopped at the surface and the more minute particles are retained deeper in the body of the filter. This is the first result produced,—it is a simple mechanical filtration. The water being cleansed of the insoluble matter, descends deeper; each particle of sand is drenched with a thin film of water; thus divided, the water offers to the confined air in the earth or filter an enormous surface of action. Now commences the second effect of perfect filtration and aeration, which is the combustion of the organic matter in solution in the water. It is a general saying that fire purifies everything, and indeed there is no organic matter, so impure or so unhealthy, which fire, with the aid of the oxygen of the air, will not transform into carbonic acid, water and nitrogen. In the interior of this filter a purification likewise takes place, not violent and visible like that caused by fire, but slow and without any perceptible evidence; nevertheless it is a combustion which reduces all organic impurities to carbonic acid, water and nitrogen. It is even a more perfect combustion than that caused by fire, producing oxydation of the nitrogen and the formation of nitric acid, a result which fire cannot produce.

"In conclusion, I will say that the filtration and aeration of all river waters would be beneficial, but as to its practicability, I beg leave to refer the subject to the consideration of those whose province it is to determine such matters."

The following extract from the New York *Tribune* refers to the recent epidemic at Plymouth, Penn.:

"The result of the investigation of the causes of the epidemic at Plymouth, Penn., made by Dr. Cyrus Edson and Dr. James B. Taylor, of the Board of Health, assisted by the chemist of the Board, Dr. Edward W. Martin, will be reported to the Board as soon as the analysis of water taken from the Susquehanna River where it flows past the town from a mountain stream, from wells, and from mines in the vicinity, are completed. The investigating physicians went to Plymouth last Wednesday and returned on Saturday. Dr. Edson yesterday told a *Tribune* reporter what they saw and what conclusions they had arrived at. He said:

"The fever prevailing at Plymouth is one of the most interesting epidemics that we have ever had in this country. The great majority of the cases have been caused by one case of typhoid fever. That case has inoculated between 700 and 1,000 cases almost simultaneously—all within the period between March 26 and April 1. No doubt the infection was spread by the water, though other causes assisted. The town was just ripe for it. The streets were filthy, and the place altogether in bad condition. The systems of the people were in a condition that made them easy victims to the disease. They had been drinking water polluted with sewage. On March 26 a new supply of water was received from a mountain stream which had been polluted by the dejections of a typhoid fever patient, who was sick in a house near the stream. They were thrown on the snow within a few feet of this water course. The snow melted and flowed into the stream, the water of which, being released by the melting of the ice that had confined it, soon filled up the reservoirs, which until then were almost empty. The water passing through the ice and hardly exposed to the air reached the reservoirs a little over one-eighth of a mile distant. The great outburst of the typhoid fever occurred between April 12 and April 18. The time of incubation of typhoid fever is generally from ten to twenty days. We looked into the milk supply carefully. A few cases were due to that, but many who had their own cows had the fever. The epidemic is now dying out. The water is all right now and was before, but it was infected by accident. The river water, although that was hardly contaminated, was pumped into the mines for several weeks prior to March 26.

"The result of the investigation only shows the necessity of keeping a water supply pure and free from contamination. The wells in this city are all worse than any in that town, where they are frequently polluted by adjacent filth. I have found people using water from wells dug in this city. I had to arrest John Gelston, a large mineral-water manufacturer, a few weeks ago for using well water in making his beverages. He was convicted in the Special Sessions and fined $25. I discovered that he was using well water by having his mineral waters analyzed. A manufacturer like him can save from $2,500 to $3,000 in Croton water taxes by using well water. Our recent investigation at the Croton water-shed shows that there is no reason for apprehension on account of the pollution of the water at present, but the population near the river bank is increasing, and after a while there will be danger unless the city purchases the land on both banks for half a mile back, or takes some other measures to prevent contamination. It would be cheaper to buy the land now than to wait until the danger is imminent and the land dearer."

Not only at Plymouth but in other towns and cities without

number, the streams run dry, or nearly so, not only in the heat of summer but in the winter months also, and everywhere "there is death in the pot." Nor is the craze to make money by manufacturing tile, having no other purpose than to hurry off the waters as fast as possible, in any degree greater, than that of the farmer who seizes upon it, paying his money for a curse rather than a blessing, and digging trenches regardless alike of expense and philosophy, begetting water famines as surely to come in time as death and the undertaker.

There is no reason why the river at Plymouth should have been dry in March, nor, indeed, during any month of any year. All the springs, brooks, rivulets and rivers of our land can be made, should be made, those of perpetual flow. Their waters should be pure and undefiled, bringing life, joy, health and happiness to the people, instead of being defiled by decay and bearing death to animal and vegetable creations.

Should the doctors continue on with the work they have undertaken, which they will surely do, they will succeed in curing nearly everybody hitherto sick, and preventing disease in the future. They have but to convince mankind that pure water is the source of health, and its opposite an equal fountain from which flows disease and death, and the world will not be long finding out that passing the waters through soils purifies them completely.

Among all who came to look over our grounds during the seasons of 1883 and '84, no one made so careful an examination into the principle of our system, as the Hon. Charles R. Earley, who has a divided residence between Philadelphia and his model hillside home at Ridgway, Elk County, Pennsylvania. We say model home, since such it cannot fail to become, should the Doctor carry out his present intentions of making application of our system to his place, demonstrating the utmost of its possibilities. To do this, would call for the use of tile, clay or cement, since, unfortunately in the light of economy, Dr. Earley is not as well situated as those who can with greater economy and facility avail themselves of the advantages of our discoveries, as he does not possess what is, in due time to be recognized as the greatest of good fortunes, a retentive subsoil coupled with an abundance of stone. Notwithstanding this the Doctor was one of the first among friends who entered heartily into sympathy with us, carefully examining our methods. A man of rare intuition he seemed to discover the whole thing at a glance, pronounced us on the right track and predicted that our work was one sure to result in making an end of the running of the waters in riot over soils; that the latter could and ultimately would be so conformed as to pass the waters of rains, dews and snows *through them*, and that waters of streams, pools, ponds and lakes would be by this means filtered and made pure, and relatively an end be made of the seeds of fungus now producing decay and death. Doctor Earley, was, in fact, the first man whom we met who agreed with us as regarded this fertile and fundamental cause, from which, come the ills to which all flesh is heir.

PHILADELPHIA, PA., March 28th, 1885.
Hon. A. N. Cole, Wellsville, N. Y.

DEAR SIR :—Your letter enclosing circular, was forwarded to me here from my home at Ridgway, Pa. I see in the circular that I am expected to write a chapter on fungi, for your forthcoming volume, devoted to the promotion of your new system of agriculture and horticulture.

This demand comes upon me like an electric shock, as I fear that the time will be too short to do justice to so important a subject. My time is so fully taken up with a diversity of interests, that I hardly know how to gain the time required to treat a subject of such prime importance, since it is one that will not bear hasty attention. The life, health and happiness of the human family depends greatly upon a full and correct understanding of the part which fungi occupies in the various diseases with which mankind is burdened. We might say that to this one cause may be traced a greater part of the diseases known to medicine. The food we eat, the water we drink, and the air we breathe are all to a greater or less extent impregnated with poisonous fungoid atoms.

To bring this chapter consistently within the scope and tenor of your volume, it will be necessary for me to go into the subject in some order and system, and to that end I will divide the matter into the following heads :

Fungi—its action on Man.

Fungi—its action on Stock Animals.

Fungi—its action on Vegetation.

Fungi—its action on Man.—Now in treating the subject under this head, I wish it understood that I do not propose to go into a technical analysis or treatise on the genera, forms, phases and nomenclature of fungi, but rather to speak of it in a general way, and of such as exert a baneful influence.

In order to investigate its action on man, it is but natural that I should examine more especially as to the vehicles that carry the deleterious cause to the circulation and tissues. It may be by inhalation, but it is certainly more frequently carried into the system by means of food and drink. That fungal spores are constantly afloat in the air, is certain, and apart from my own investigations, I could cite a number of reliable authorities.

The experiments of Dr. Cunningham, conducted in India, have been convincing on this point............*"Spores and other vegetable cells are constantly present in the atmospheric dust, and

---

*From microscopic Examinations of Air, from the 9th Annual Report of the Sanitary Commission. Calcutta, 1872.

usually occur in considerable numbers; the majority of them are living and capable of growth and development."

"Recently a case occurred at the Botanic Gardens at Edinburgh, which was somewhat novel. The assistant to the Botanical professor was preparing for demonstration some dried specimens of a large puff-ball, filled with the dustlike spores, which he accidentally inhaled, and was for sometime confined to his room under medical attendance from the irritation they caused."*

This seemingly is an endorsement that the air we breathe is at all times more or less charged with fungal material, which under certain conditions is capable of development to such an extent as to cause local irritation, and as I well know, from personal experience and investigation, will at times produce blood poisoning with its train of concomitant evils.

Commencing the practice of medicine at the age of twenty-two, I devoted my best energies to that profession, during a period of about forty years. In April, 1846, I left my native state, New York, and settled in the wilds of upper Pennsylvania, where the nearest physician was forty miles away. I was thus alone in my struggle with those enemies of man,—death and disease. To my surprise I found, that there was hardly a man, woman or child in that whole region in perfect health. On the mountains and hillsides, in the valleys, and in the towns, I found that nearly everyone was in some way diseased.

This was to my mind an anomalous condition of affairs, and being of an investigating turn of mind, I sought in every instance, where I was called upon to attend the sick, to trace its cause. I said to myself, here is my work, which must call forth my full energies. Here begins the work of the doctor, which never has, can or will end; to examine into the remote and latent cause of

---

*Fungi. M. C. Cooke, M. A., L. L. D.

disease. It is not only the duty of the physician to help nature in the cure of disease, but it is also part of his work to seek out and remove the primary cause. He must examine the dwelling inside and out, the cellar beneath, the food the family eat; the water they drink and the air they breathe. In fact it is preëminently his duty to *prevent* as well as *cure* disease.

It is requisite in investigating for a first cause, that the physician should examine closely into the modes and ways and living of the people immediately surrounding the patient. One great cause of disease of the people with whom I was brought in contact, was the ill-advised custom of storing their winter supply of vegetables and provisions in the cellars of their houses. It is a fact demonstrated beyond the possibility of a doubt, that such a thing as perfectly healthy fruit or vegetable is rarely to be found. The undetected incipient potatoe rot has frequently done its work of death by the production of blood poison. It is almost impossible to find an unblemished apple, pear, peach, plum, cherry or berry. They all have spots or blemish of some kind, and wherever you find fermentation and decay, you will also find fungi.

The fungi as germs of disease are always present both in the air and food. Go to a market, tell the fruit dealer that you want a bushel of apples without speck or blemish, and that for that bushel you will give him the price of a barrel. His answer to you will be:

"I could not do that sir, for the price of four barrels, and I doubt if I could do it at all."

This is not only the case with fruit, but with all vegetables and cereals.

Now in view of all this, is it not patent that we are constantly taking the germs of disease? Most assuredly it is. Our circulation and tissues are full of disease-bearing germs, only awaiting full development and opportunity to do their fell work. Why, when I think of it in all its details, I am only surprised there is not more sickness and death. Surprised that there should be any apparently well people anywhere. Most people eat their food without a thought as to whether it is pure and healthy, or that diseased food can not do otherwise than produce diseased and poisonous blood. Go into the gardens of our towns, and those out in the country, and examine the growing vegetables. How many of them will you find in a healthy condition? I think you will fail to find one single plant that is perfect. Either the roots, stalk, leaf or fruit will be found affected in some way. Take the water we drink. It will not take long, nor will you need the aid of a powerful microscope, to convince you of the presence of fungi, or germs of some kind.

Fungi—its action on stock animals.

As man is only a higher type of animal, it is but natural, that that which affects him, will also affect the lower animals; the only difference being that of degree. That which would probably be very virulent in man, would be of a milder type in the other. Then too the type of its manifestation might be different, but the same first cause will be always present. Poisoned blood and tissues produced by poisoned food, water and air. But there is another feature that is generally overlooked. There is not so much care used in selecting their food and water as is the case with man. If the bran or corn meal happens to be a little musty, sour or wormy, it is not thrown away. No; it is fed to the stock. They will not notice it. If the sides of the water trough are green with slime, it is not thoroughly cleansed. They will drink. Cattle are not fastidious. If the hay is a little musty, it is not discarded. The stock have not very discriminating eyes, they will eat it. If the air of the stables reek with ammoniacal gas and have little or no ventilation, it matters not. The animals do not notice it, or if they do, they can not remonstrate. But here let me ask, are the people not being surely punished? I think the reply to this would be unanimously affirmative were we able to follow the effect that the manures from these animals have on the food cereals brought to fruition through its use. Not only the human family is suffering from this terrible condition and neglect of our soil, thus producing fungi, but our stock animals are suffering in an equally bad way. The grasses that they feed from in our pastures, and the hay made from same and stored for winter use, if examined under a microscope, will be found to be extensively covered with fungi. This bears various titles, such as smut, rust, or mildew, or other names applied in different localities. Corn, in many sections, is sowed for fodder, and this, upon examination, will be found to be in the same condition. In this connection I would refer to the recent developments in Texas, where cattle were suffering with what a number of authorities pronounced contagious pleuro-pneumonia; but upon investigation, were found to be in a diseased condition, from eating of corn that was extensively smutted. Oats with their rust, wheat and rye with their ergot and other diseases, all these different productions are alike affected.

Our writers on the subject of stock, refer frequently to (so-called) contagious pleuro-pneumonia. Cows kept for their milk for supplying our large cities and towns, are nearly all fed with this mass of poison, and kept in badly ventilated stables, shut up and excluded from the air. Congress and our legislatures pass laws and appoint commissioners to examine into and destroy all stock affected, to prevent the spread of the contagion. They never for one moment think of examining the farms and stables, and the feed of the animal. In my investigations in the vicinity of Philadelphia, into "contagious pleuro pneumonia" (so-called.)

I found diseased mucous membrane, the air passages thickened, congestion of the lining membranes, all more or less congested and covered with slime and fungi, so much so indeed, that the smaller tubes of the bronchials were collapsed, thus preventing free passage of air, consequently making it impossible to fully inflate the lungs. Not only were the bronchials affected, but I also found the throat and mouth extensively covered with slime and fungi. On examining into the character of the food which had been fed I found that, in many cases, it consisted of malt dust, full of fungi. Garbage in some cases was fed, and many different kinds of food supposed to produce milk rapidly. The grass and hay in almost every case, I found to contain mould or fungi in some form.

Is there such a disease as "Contagious Pleuro-Pneumonia?"

I clip the following from the morning papers of Philadelphia, of Saturday, June 6th, 1885.

[*From the Record.*]

"Much excitement has been occasioned among the farmers in the vicinity of Pavonia on the northern outskirts of Camden by the appearance of the pleuro-pneumonia in the herd of cattle on the farm of M. Feenfer. Drs. Miller and Dyer of the State Board of Health have investigated the outbreak and believe that the rigid quarantine which they have established will prevent the spread of the disease. The herd of nine cows was purchased last February at the West Philadelphia stock yards. Two of the infected animals have been killed and the remainder inoculated."

[*From the Times.*]

"A general examination is being made of herds of cattle in Camden and Gloucester Counties by Drs. W. B. E. Miller and C. K. Dyer, of the New Jersey State Board of Health. On the farm of M. Feenfer, at Pavonia, near the Camden Water Works, a herd of fine cattle is said to be infected with pleuro-pneumonia. The disease was brought to the farm by three or four cows which were purchased by Mr. Feenfer at the West Philadelphia stock yard in February last. Great care will be taken by the authorities to prevent the spread of the disease and the herd has been quarantined."

Having had some experience in investigating the causes of diseases in both man and beast pronounced as "contagious" by many, which to my mind were caused by bad food, bad air and bad drink, I at once went to Camden, N. J., where we procured a conveyance and were taken to the "farm" referred to above, near Pavonia, a distance of about three miles from the City Hall, Camden. There are about fifty dwellings scattered about this place. On our way there we met the two veterinary surgeons or members of the State Board of Health, Drs. Miller and Dyer returning from the "Feenfer farm" where they had been visiting the sick cows. On our arrival at Michael Feenfer's place about 10 o'clock A. M., we found Mr. Feenfer the "farmer" referred to was away with his milk wagon selling the milk from the cows not yet dead or dying, and would not return before 11.30, so we were introduced to his son, a young man about 17 years old, who very kindly showed us all the surroundings of the place.

The "farm" referred to consisted of about four town lots on which were erected, one dwelling house, and outhouses, one cow stable, one cow shed, a hogpen and a hen-house, situated about one-half mile from the Delaware River on rather low ground.

We found the stable about sixteen by twenty-four feet, with eight stalls on each side, three feet wide. The door opened out into the cow shed which was about the same size as the stable and open on one side. The stable was low and had loose boards placed overhead where hay was kept for feed. There was also a window that opened out into the yard, which window and door were the only means of ventilation provided.

Just in front of this window and door was a cesspool about fifteen feet in diameter that took up the drainage and filth from the cow stable, hogpen and hen-house, as well as the drainage from the dwelling and all the outhouses. This cesspool was full of the very worst of filth. The liquid was as black as tar and they had recently filled it with swamp and bog sods, with long swamp weeds and grass, as they said "to keep the cows from miring." In the stable was found but one cow, the rest of the stalls were full of all sorts of trash and filth. The shed was in like condition, only worse. We opened up our inquiries as follows:

"How many cows have you?"

"We had thirteen."

"How many have you now?"

"Six and this sick one."

"What became of the others?"

"Four died, one we sold and one we gave away."

"Where are the six?"

"In the pasture."

"How did your cows get sick?"

"We bought one cow from the West Philadelphia stock yard about two months ago and in about a week after we bought her she had a calf, and in about two days after she had her calf, she took sick and died. The cow doctors said she caught the disease in the stock yard."

"Did the calf get sick and die?"

"No, the calf was healthy."

"What did you do with the calf?"

"We sold the calf to the butchers."

"Were there any cows sick in the stock yard when you bought this one?"

"Not as we can learn."

DIAGRAM OF STABLES AND OUTHOUSES.

"Had there been any sick before or has there been any sick there since?"

"No, not as we can learn."

"How many acres of land have you in your farm?"

"We have no land only these lots. We rent pasture."

"How many acres do you rent?"

"We rent about three acres for pasture and pay sixty-five dollars for it."

We now looked at the sick cow. The young man opened her mouth, and upon looking in we found the mucous membrane of the throat and nostrils much congested and somewhat inflamed with but little drenling or slabbering. She had no cough or difficulty in breathing. She did not get up.

We then went to see the cows in the pasture. This pasture bordered upon a swamp next to the river and was about twenty to thirty feet wide and bounded on the other side by a deep swale which was again bounded by a swamp over half a mile long. This strip of land was divided in the middle by an embankment or dike which kept out the tide from the marsh land.

Therefore there was but this strip of land about fifteen feet wide and a little over a half mile long that could be utilized for pasture. But no grass was to be seen, save a few roots here and there, and these nearly covered by the droppings from the cows. They have no other water to drink except that from the swamp which was nearly as black as ink. These six cows were put out there after the others died and were kept there night and day. They were placed there by order of the members of the State Board of Health as above (the Feenfers called them the "cow-doctors") and quarantined. They are fed with malt grains, etc., as hereafter explained, drink the swamp water and breathe the swamp air.

On returning to the stable we found Mr. Michael Feenfer the

"farmer," had reached home. He was a very pleasant German and showed us the feed which they called "malt grains and other stuff." There was a large hogshead standing under the before described cow-shed, just in front of the door of the stable which was about two-thirds full of malt grains and other material, so sour and stinking that one could not look into it without getting sick. On asking the old man "if the cows liked that kind of food," he said, "sometimes they acted as if they did not and it made them cough sometimes.

We inquired as to how much milk they got from the cows, and he said they got one hundred and twenty quarts from the thirteen, but now they got about sixty-five from the six. We asked, "how much do you get from the sick cow at a milking?" He said "about a pint, and that they fed to the hogs.

"How many hogs have you?"

"We have but five now, two died last fall."

"What was the matter of the hogs that died?"

"They got sick just like the cows, the five are pretty well now."

Now let us look at this matter clearly, in the light of reason and science and what do we find? Brutes suffering. Human ignorance. Legalized cruelty to dumb animals. Woful want of intelligent investigation, wilful disregard of the very first principles of hygiene.

It hardly seems possible that any one with the slightest degree of intelligence could make any mistake as to where the primary cause of all this sickness laid. Here was a depression or hole made in the ground that caught all the surface drainage for say two hundred feet around it. All the wash-water from the houses drained into it, all the filth from the stable and pig-pen drained into it, every rain washed through the hen-house into it. There was absolutely no exit for the water. There it was, dammed up, with all the excrement and vegetable matter that could be imagined, slowly putrifying and throwing off noxious gasses and vapors. The cows were confined in stables that had no means of ventilation save the door, and one window, *opening out upon this pool of filth.*

The food they got came from this hogshead of malt grains and other garbage in a high state of fermentation. This reeking mass of stuff was given to support life and make milk. The smell at a distance of ten feet was enough to turn any stomach.

This is a graphic but true pen picture of the home life of these cows. Now the cows are sick and ailing. They must be taken out to pasture. Mark the keen sarcasm, unintentional it is true,—these animals gain one thing by the change,—sunlight. They must eat of the rank marsh grass and drink of the fetid marsh water. I noticed fish in the sluices; but in this marsh water there are none. It's pretty bad water that a catfish won't swim in.

Now taking the character of their food, the air and water into consideration, is it any wonder that these cattle should have diseases of the throat and lungs? It is a wonder that they have any healthy organs at all, and I doubt if they have.

Mark the ignorant way in which the State Inspector does his work. Did he do as we did? Did he look for a cause upon the premises? No, he contented himself by asking the nearly as ignorant "farmer,"—"What made your cows sick?" and upon receiving the reply caught at the pretext,—Ah! that is it, you got them from the stock yard. Yes, yes, she brought the infection with her.

Upon looking up the matter it is impossible to find that any of the stock at the stock yard was sick with this disease either before or after this cow was purchased. Now, is it likely that the so-called infection was brought from the stock yard? Is it not a hundred times more likely that the bad air, bad water, and bad feed at the farm induced this disease?

The gases that rise from decaying manure are exceedingly poisonous. The urine from stables of stock contains much more putrescent matter than manure does, and is therefore more dangerous.

Now, as in the case just mentioned, where there is a hollow in the stable-yard, which hollow is not drained, it becomes the receptacle for all the waste that is around the place. The drainage from the house, pigpens, and stables drain into it. There is no outlet and it must remain there, only to find an exit in evaporation. The animal and vegetable matter settles down in it, fermentation begins and is hastened by the heat of the sun. Now when evaporating, the particles of humidity rise from the bottom of this pile of corruption, thus producing a current which carries with it the products of putrefaction. These products are sometimes parasitic in their nature. They float in the air, settle on the surface of the water, and sift into the food. When taken into the lungs by inspiration, they find resting places in the membranes, where with an even temperature of sufficient height to bring them to active life disease results. The same thing occurs when taken into the stomach in food and drink. In the first instance they cause diseases of the mouth, throat and lungs, in the latter, their effects are noted in derangement of the stomach and bowels.

Should we be asked whether there is any way of avoiding this condition of affairs, we unhesitatingly would point you out the real reason for all the trouble, and at the same time suggest the cure. First comes, *fermentation*, then *decomposition*, the production of fungi in all its forms, and of course this must be followed by *disease*.

Now to my mind Nature intended that the ground should have air to breathe and water to drink, just the same as animals. It needs these, not so much for supplying nutriment to vegetation, as it does to carry on the great work of assimilation and purification. Is it not true that all decomposition and filth is converted into innocuous material in nature's laboratory? And if so, is it not directly caused by fermentation and oxidation? It is burnt and calcined into purity. The earth being loose and porous, the air forces its way into the crevices, and the water passes through it from above, each, especially the air, supplying fuel to carry on the work of purification.

We will suppose that the water comes to a strata that is impervious to its onward course. What happens? Simply this,—it dams up slowly, inch by inch, forcing out the air as it goes. All motion and circulation is stopped. Fermentation and decomposition soon begin. The earth is drowned out—suffocated,—dead for want of air. How is this? Water is good for the ground? Yes, but not in this way, the water must be moving constantly. There must be a current of air and water and not too much or too little of the latter.

This very much desired result can very readily be obtained by seeking a water level and proper drainage and full control of the water so that air can follow and leaven through the earth; so also, that God's most blessed earth reviver—rain and the dews—may circulate through it, so that the old water may not for an instant rest and start fermentation, always on and away, so that there may be plenty of oxygen coming down into its pores, seeking and burning out all filth and corruption. To sum up concisely:

Use Cole's system of capillary irrigation as patented by him. Thus you get clear of all filth and corruption that is found in these miserable cesspools,—they never form.

You filter all water wherever it strikes the soil from the clouds and other places and localities. You convert even what is so much contaminated with organic matter and other impurities into pure water and hold it back in time of over supply, heavy rainfalls and melting snows, for the use of the soil and vegetation as the wants of each may require.

Should this system be adopted by farmers and dairy-men such diseases as the so-called "contagious pleuro-pneumonia" and other fatal diseases among stock will be wholly unknown, only adding ventilation and stopping the feeding of garbage and decayed and fermented foods and fungi.

On many of the smaller farms grass or hay is raised and stored away without careful treatment. Fresh manure is frequently hauled from city stables, and spread over land to ferment and rot. Upon examination, the class of lands thus treated, are found covered with fungi in the shape of devils-bread, puff-ball, toadstools and others of different names. Bone dust and other fertilizers are also used. Then come the wet spells, and the dry spells, and the hot spells, which together keep up a continual fermentation in the soil about the roots of crops and grasses. We find in many sections of the country, places where they raise stock, particularly hogs. These animals are turned into the orchards in the fall or late summer, and permitted to eat of the fallen fruit. They are therefore allowed to eat freely of rotten and fungi-covered food, and, again, are fed upon slops, swill and all manners of filth. As a consequence, we hear from many parts of the country of hog cholera. In all these cases our lawmakers, authorities, and societies for the prevention of cruelty to animals, have never been known to open their mouths against this worst of all cruelties to the dumb animals. Their food is fed them only to their destruction. That which should nourish poisons. Bad food, bad water, and bad air alike, contribute to their destruction. While poisoned food is not only chargeable to fungi, there is also the decaying vegetables in our cellars and surroundings, constantly contaminating and poisoning the air with its foulness which we are obliged to breathe. Thus we have malaria as it is called. This without doubt comes from decaying vegetable matter, whether it be from sewers, streets, swamps, or from our own vegetable stores, laid away for winter use. The custom of spreading fresh manure over our lands to rot and ferment, throwing off noxious gasses, is another fruitful cause of malaria.

Fungi—its action on vegetation.

While I have divided the subject into three heads for the better handling of it, yet are they so closely allied in their effects one upon the other, as to admit of really very little difference. Under this last head, we come to a field exceedingly vast, and one over which, at the best, can take but a cursory glance. Even had I the time to devote to it, I fear it to be too great in extent to go into it in detail. That it is a field abounding in speculation, yet fraught with vast importance no one can deny. It is of so much importance as to cause me to hesitate at beginning, as to whether I had not better put it first in order, instead of last. Under this will be found the fountain head of all the trouble.

The dry rot has destroyed, without doubt, many thousands of dollars worth of valuable timber. We know that in turning the soil, we frequently find a stringy, gummy mass of fungi, that runs its tentacle like arms in every direction like those of the cuttle fish. This it has been proved interferes sadly with the growth of plants, grasses and trees. Almost all of the cereals and grasses suffer from fungi in some shape. Rust, smut, mildew and caries are nearly always present.

Now is there any remedy? Is there any way to prevent this constant promotion, production, and spread of disease bearing fungi?

You may remember, in the last of June, 1883, while I was in

Wellsville, that I was invited in company with the Hon. T. L. Minier, Hon. S. L. Taber, Hon. John H. Selkreg and others, to dine with you at your home on the hillside. At your table, we were much astonished to see the most delicious fresh peas just picked from the vines, and the finest strawberries that all acknowledged ever having seen. The question was asked :

"Where do you get such fine peas?" Your answer was : "they were picked from my own garden."

"Where do you get such berries?"

"They are also picked from my own garden."

"Come now, Mr. Cole, that will never do," I said, "I was raised in Allegany County. This is too early in the season for either peas or strawberries. Besides, Allegany never produced such peas and berries as these."

Your reply was, that this was the fruit of your system of underground irrigation. You then explained to us your system of sinking troughs in the ground, and taking up the water as it fell, and holding it back, to supply moisture to vegetation as it was required. This was entirely a new feature to us all, and after dinner, we repaired to your garden, a lot on the hillside, where you explained to us your system in detail. The more I examined, the more I was astonished to find every bush, twig, stalk, tree and fruit perfectly clean and healthy. No rust or fungi of any kind whatsoever was to be found. You showed us a stream of water coming from the trenches, a continuous, bright and sparkling brook, and yet, it was a dry time ; quite a drouth. But in spite of all this, we found a stream of water coming from your hillside constantly, with no spring to feed it, only coming from the stored up rains and dews that fell, caught up and garnered by these troughs, furnishing a constant vapor to the roots of your vegetables and plants, keeping them in uniform condition of moisture ;

never too wet, never too dry. This system made a very deep impression upon me, and upon returning home and thinking the matter over, you will remember I wrote you a letter, suggesting that by the use of natural gas (which must take the place of coal and wood for heating purposes) to heat the water in the Fall and Spring, and running steam pipes through the troughs, (or dropping the warm water into them) to keep the water warm, you might raise all kinds of produce, and as it were, do away with winter. You could do, as I found while in Europe was done there, produce the finest pineapples by use of this warm water system, thus doing away with expensive hot houses. In this letter I also suggested, that, where you wished to raise tropical fruits, you could throw a canvass over the space, to keep off the winds and snows. All this was in the most part a joke, as applied to Allegany, but upon receiving your reply, I was astounded to read that you had already obtained a patent covering these points.

On the second day of July last, I was again in Wellsville. In passing through the streets, I noticed on the corner baskets of strawberries; some were small, diseased looking berries, but alongside of them were luscious ones, nearly as large as peaches. Said I :

"How much are your strawberries?"

"These are sold at thirteen cents; and these at twenty-five a quart," was the answer made by the vender.

"But why should there be such a difference in price?" I inquired.

"Why! these are Cole's berries."

"Cole's berries! What do you mean by Cole's berries?"

"Why! they are raised here in town, by Mr. Cole."

"Who is Mr. Cole?"

"What! don't you know A. N. Cole?"

"Oh! yes; he has been termed the father of the Republican

party. So he raised these berries here in town. Well, I do know A. N. Cole, and I think he has succeeded in raising better strawberries than children, for let me tell you, that his Republican children have given us Democrats a mighty sight of trouble."

"Yes, sir; that is so. He generally succeeds with anything he undertakes."

"How many of those berries does it take to make a quart?"

"About twenty to thirty; I suppose an average of twenty-five would cover it."

"Why! you had better sell them for a cent apiece."

"Well, they sell at that as fast as lightning. They don't stay on hand long."

Of course I knew whose berries they were, as soon as I saw them. It was only a whim of mine to interview the groceryman.

The next day a party of us were visiting your grounds, and you may well remember the liberties taken by me at that time. I then had with me a powerful glass, and I was determined to investigate matters thoroughly. I examined the roots, leaves, stalks and berries of your strawberry vines. I dissected and investigated them in every imaginable way, as also the pea vines, cauliflower, cabbage, and in fact all vegetables and vegetation within your grounds; and as I told you at that time, I did not find a single exception, wherein a plant was not perfectly clean and healthy. No fungi to be found anywhere. Root, stalk, leaf, twig and fruit all in perfect health, and absolutely free from fungus or parasites. Strawberries larger than plums; and everything in like proportion. Even the timothy and other grasses seemed brighter, fresher and more luxuriant.

Of course, I enquired into the expense per acre of such a system, which I cannot pretend to give from memory; I will leave that to you. But allow me to say, that if all lands were, in place of underdraining and subsoiling, treated as you do yours; deep trenches broad and wide, filled with stones, and covered with soil as yours are; fertilized with a compost as you prepare it; having it fully assimilated before using—I say, if all this could be done, then, and not till then, can we do away with this creation, cultivation and dissemination of poisonous fungi, which, as has been shown, is working such sad disaster and death to the whole animal and vegetable world.

A few pages back I asked the question, whether the people were not being punished for the bad treatment their stock was receiving. Now let us see if they are not. We spread out over our fields the manure coming from these animals. If they happen to have any disease, their excrement is sure to have more or less germs in it of the same disease. The manure lies upon the ground, and is subjected to the action of the wet and heat, and the chemical influence is imparted to the soil. Now the soil is too wet, now to dry; there is no happy medium. At one time it is a mass of mud, at others it is baked like a brick. There is no golden mean. At all events, there is a constant state of fermentation going on. If the materials employed could be completely rotted, there would probably not be so much harm done; but where you have vegetable matter only partly rotted, you are positively sure to produce fungi. This again fastens on the grasses and other products, which are in turn, fed to man and stock. Can any sane man for an instant doubt, that this continuous production and consumption of fungi, is not bound to produce the most disastrous results. Must this disease producing system go on forever in the same channel? Must no one raise the voice of warning, and call attention to it? Must no one point with pregnant finger to the signs of its fell work? Are not the facts spread out that "he who runs may read?" Oh!

farmers and truckers, if you will not be warned for humanity's sake, take heed and notice the conversation had between myself and the groceryman. The price of the healthy berries was twice that of the poor ones. If the good of mankind will not move you to pity and a change of method, let your pockets plead with you. Try the experiment, as tried at the "Home on the Hillside," and see if your wallets will not be considerably distended, and the lives and health of yourselves and families preserved and lengthened.

Yours Truly,   C. R. EARLEY.

Such cities as Philadelphia, Pa., Syracuse, Elmira, and Binghamton, in N. Y., Paterson, N. J., Wilmington, Del., and others we might mention are situated on what are called river bottoms, and yet, so far above high water mark, as to make drainage into rivers not only easy, but perfect. Whether, for the systems of sewerage already arranged, our methods could be substituted we cannot at present decide, but have no doubt of its practicability. That the municipal authorities of towns and cities thus located, could be induced to make the change, is doubtful. In all portions of Europe, beneath the dwellings in cities, towns and villages, on the grounds of kings and nobility, and those of the peasant and the pauper, the damps and decays generative of disease, bringing death before its time, are found. The same is relatively true of the older cities of our own country. But younger cities and towns are increasing in population, and new ones continually developing, and with these at least, an effort should be made to obtain a pure water supply. The fact is distressing and astonishing that such cities as St. Paul, Detroit and thousands of others, developed and developing in different portions of our country, should have no provision made for conserving the rains and snows falling upon the roofs of dwellings, barns, stables and other structures, or running off from the lawns, gardens and grounds of the people.

Keeping watch of the measures proposed and methods being adopted to purify the waters, and add sufficiently to the supply of Croton to furnish the City of New York with at least five times the present amount of good drinking water, we knew to a mathematical certainty that it could be accomplished if the water that falls annually in the form of rains, dews and snows was preserved. We also knew full well that the possibilities of our system were not reached when, nearly two years ago, the Hon. Warner Miller, having looked somewhat into this question of saving, purifying and utilizing these waters remarked as follows:

"I confess to being unprepared for your claims, Mr. Cole, and yet, if what you anticipate can be only partially realized, the State of New York alone, is capable of sustaining a population of one hundred millions."

The Senator alluded more particularly to Herkimer County and the Mohawk River, great, if not the greatest among counties, and grand among the grandest of our rivers, now moving turbidly on, its waters as unlike those of an hundred years ago as clay is unlike crystal. What is true of the Mohawk, is equally true as applied to nearly all the rivers of the older settled portions of our country. The waters of these are filled with roil for a large portion of the year, and are always polluted; our springs are dried up, and when not wholly so, their waters mix and mingle with drains in which death and decay widespread and prevailing, are borne by rains into the streams supplying towns and cities with water for cooking and drinking purposes.

We have known for years, that, unless means are provided for fitting and rendering the waters of these rivers and their tributaries pure, fungus, deadliest enemy of vegetable and animal life, would go on with its work of decimation and death, and not only the fish would die out and disappear, but disease everywhere would increase, and our people, more especially those dwelling in large towns and cities, would not live out half the days allotted to man. Equally well had we become satisfied that the stagnation of the waters could be provided against and by passing them through soils, they could be purified and rendered crystal clear and cool; kept from freezing in winter and held sufficiently cool in summer, to be more grateful and healthful than ice water.

CHAPTER VI.

RECLAIMING THE GREAT AMERICAN DESERT.

Months ago an article appeared in the *Scientific American* from the pen of Professor John Le Conte, on the subject of the arid regions of our country, commonly called the Great American desert. Not possessing a file of the paper and having preserved only a mere scrap of this article, we are unable to quote more than the following:

"A vast treeless region, stretching away from the eastern base of the Rocky Mountains and the great plains, plateaus and basins lying west of the same range, and constituting the arid region, embracing more than one third of the entire area within the territorial boundaries of the American Union."

After giving a description of this vast desert, Professor Le Conte proceeds to show such conditions existing as to make the lands of this region only productive by means of irrigation, and gives it as his opinion that, were every spring, rill, rivulet and lake of this entire region made available, not more than three per cent of the desert could be reclaimed. We had solved at the time this article came under our eye the problem of the conservation of the waters, and were not, in any degree, disheartened on account of this gloomy picture, but rather greatly encouraged by the fact that the Professor re-enforced our previous knowledge by his account of the great water preserves of this section—the ices and snows lying upon the summits of the mountains or within the great basins, during most of the summer period of each year. Often had our mind dwelt upon the wastes of war, and after finding out the way of the waters, we frequently reverted to the fact that, if the money spent during the last half century in the support of armies and navies, and the prosecution of wars, had been diverted to constructing a canal along the northern incline of the African Continent, dropping the waters coming of the melting of snows on the Mountains of the Moon down upon the Sahara, this great desert of Africa might have been made to blossom as the rose.

In our earliest childhood we noted that the spring smoked in midwinter, and that evaporation went on amid frosts. We had dug earth worms for fishing in the neighborhood of springs when the ground was still frozen only a few feet away, and all through life we had kept our eye on the grass green growing as the snows of winter melted about the spring. Dakota's great wheat fields, with their deep laid foundations of frost, had not escaped attention, and the warm suns of March and April shining upon these fields and bringing early germination and steady growth until harvest time, told the story of the waters beneath at spring water temperature. Nor had the conditions along the Alps and Appenines escaped our attention, where, underlying in pockets of soil, the water coming of melting snows, furnished not only moisture for the vine, but inspiration to its growth. Authentic information had been received of such an increase of production and improvement in flavor of the fruit of the vine, as to convince us that the same simple methods might be made use of to transform the arid regions of our own country into those of boundless fertility and wealth.

That our great desert is a treeless region, or one nearly so, is true, nor can it ever be otherwise until the time shall come for husbanding the waters, and making use of them in a way to prevent penetration of the frost to the depth to which they descend under existing conditions. That the reserve coming of melting ices and snows would prove efficient for this purpose if halted, held back and permitted to find their way into the valleys through the soils of this vast region, rather than over and along them as hitherto, there is no doubt in our mind. Deep trenching would doubtless become necessary, since to drop the waters below the frost line it would perhaps become imperative to sink the trenches to a depth of five or six feet. That this work will be done at a comparatively early day we have but little doubt. A few acres deep trenched upon the treeless mountain sides of Montana, Dakota or Wyoming, would tell the story. In this way, and this only, can forest and fruit trees be grown and the prairies, plains, valleys and mountain sides be clothed with that wilderness of wealth found primeval in the Atlantic regions, and indispensable to permanent prosperity.

But here comes in the question, who shall begin the work, or, once begun, by whom or by what means shall it be pushed forward? That the United States Government, coöperated with and aided by great railroad companies, to which grants have been made of lands so extensive as to appear to the ordinary observer acts of prodigality, should enter at once upon the work of reclaiming the desert, is so evident as to scarcely call for argument. In Mr. Stewart's book, page 166, from which we again quote, is found the following:

"Irrigation of land is an art that has existed for many centuries previous to any authentic written history. The traditions of the Chinese people are very ancient, and irrigation is mentioned in their earliest history, as extensively practiced. In Egypt, Syria, and the ancient kingdoms of Eastern Asia, agriculture depended almost wholly upon irrigation, and still so depends in these countries, where the people have survived the political changes of thousands of years.

"The irrigation of gardens, vineyards, and fields, is frequently referred to in the Scriptures; one of the earliest books speaks of it, and one of the prophets refers to 'furrows of the plantation.' And so agriculture has continued to the present day, the necessities of the majority of cultivators of the soil in the Eastern Hemisphere, and the natural opportunities possessed by them, continuing to render the system vital to their existence. When the Spaniards occupied the new found continent, they introduced their system of irrigation wherever the dryness of the climate demanded it.

"In Chili, Peru, Central America and Mexico, the canals and ditches made by the early Spanish settlers remain, and many are still in use. The systems adopted in California, Texas, New Mexico and Colorado are mainly copied from the ancient models. It is hardly necessary to say that these models are not of the best construction, nor at all satisfactory to the engineer of the present day, but they are cheap and easy of construction. The settlement of the drier regions of our territory, adds another instance to those of past history of the reclamation of the deserts by irrigation. It will be of interest to glance over what has already been done in this way, before considering possibilities of the future. The actual history of irrigation in the United States begins with the construction of the Pacific railroads. In the course of a few years, a great impetus was given to the settlement of lands adjacent to the rivers, and which could be brought under irrigation, and several extensive works were constructed."

Here follows an enumeration of many canals of great length, cost and capacity, and their endless adjuncts, by which thousands of acres have been, in the aggregate, reclaimed, and from having been an utter waste made more productive than an equal area in

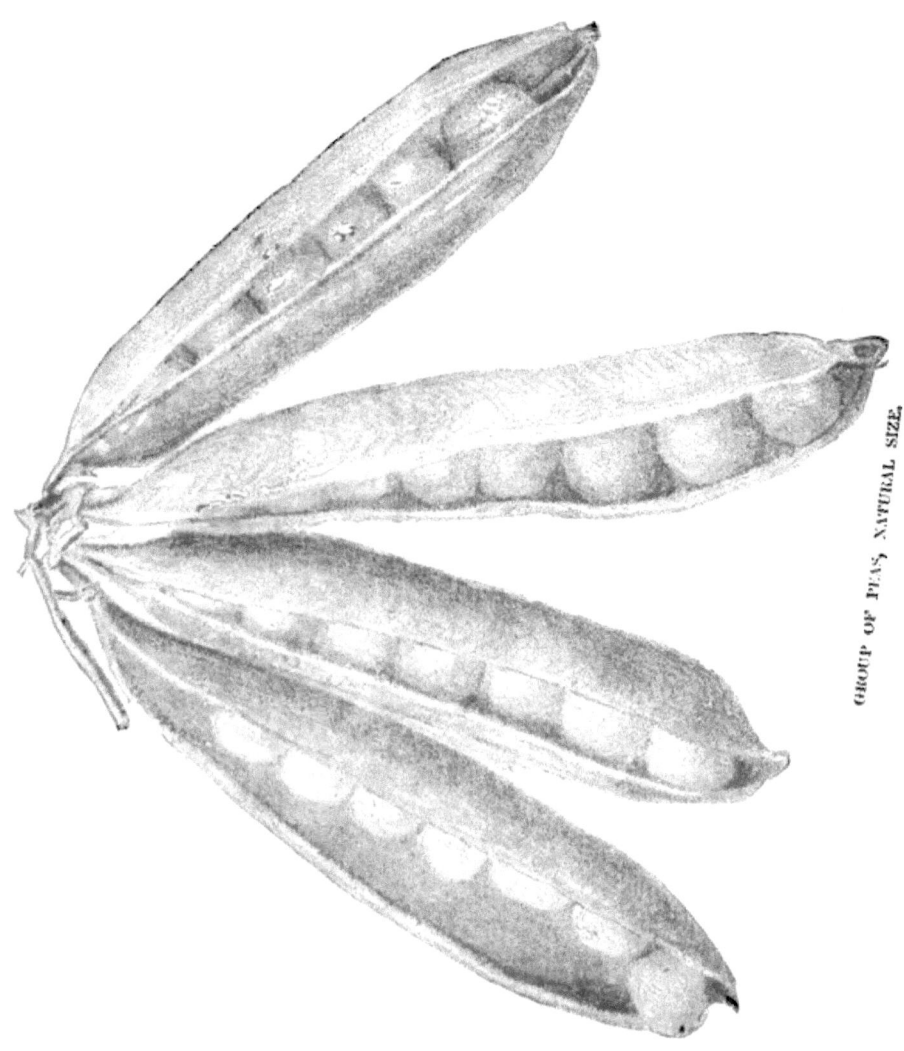

GROUP OF PEAS, NATURAL SIZE.

regions of rainfall. What is more marvelous is the fact, that what has been accomplished in this direction has been done by individual and corporate enterprise. That companies constructing these works have made money is true in a majority of instances, and happy should everybody be on account of it. The corporations and individuals who have had the fortitude to act as pioneers, have been the greatest of benefactors. Even Brigham Young and his polygamous church of Latter Day Saints, have not proven an unmitigated scourge. Great good has come out of a Nazareth, which, in certain of its aspects, presents the features of the Sodom and Gomorrah of the present age. Merest beginning has however been made.

Our "New Agriculture" dates not only a new era in irrigation, but is sure to date one equally new in government policies. The old saw "Uncle Sam is rich enough to give us all a farm," is in all probability soon to be verified in a way, which scarcely one in a million of the American people have yet dreamed. While kings and nobles of the Old World are quite generally looking to war as a means of employment for their pauper classes, and the lazaroni seem equally inclined to prefer the chances of death on battle fields and in camps, to lives of toil without sufficient remuneration to make life worth the living, an opportunity presents itself to our government and people to do that which will give employment and bring to the present and future generations more of real wealth than all the mines of the earth contain.

The unthinking citizen and the conscienceless demagogue alike, have been clamoring of late for acts of practical confiscation of the lands granted to companies to aid in construction of lines of railway across the continent. We do not hesitate to say that forfeiture of some of the grants should be made. This is nevertheless the exception to that rule of law and logic which forbids government from so far disregarding its own deliberate act, as to hold individuals and corporations to arbitrary compliance with the letter of acts under which grants have been made. The railroad company, dependent upon the sale of its lands and disposition of its stocks and bonds, is hardly dealt by when government, from having been its patron and promoter, turns about and becomes a bear to destroy its credit and bring upon its ward distress and disaster akin to ruin.

That our government can make millions of dollars for the people, by entering upon a system of reclamation covering the more hopeful portions of its desert lands, is so manifest, as to make argument to prove it unnecessary. No longer ago than 1873, under an act of Congress, approved March 3rd of that year, a commission was organized to examine the great valleys of California, with reference to construction of a system of irrigation. The report of this commission will be found in the yearly volume of the Department of Agriculture for 1874. Commenting on this report Mr. Stewart remarks :

"The conclusions reached may be seriously questioned in many points, but on the whole are, as might have been expected, favorable, both to the profitableness and feasibility of irrigation works, and to the interference of the national and state governments, and their control over the distribution of the water."

Commenting further, Mr. Stewart proceeds to say :

"By no other authority could the conflicting interests of miners, agriculturists and owners of lands to be injured or benefited by the enterprise, be properly reconciled. In Europe, the supreme control is exercised by, and the ownership of the water vested in, the State. The French government in 1669, by special law, reserved the ownership of all rivers and streams, and grants concessions to irrigating companies under certain restrictions. In Italy, the State has always exercised this ownership, and in Venice the springs and even the rainfall, so far as it can be stored in reservoirs, have been held to be public property. In India the springs and rainfall are accumulated in reservoirs controlled by the government, and the river systems are also owned by it. Not only this, but the details of the distribution of the water are also directed by government officials. This is made necessary, however, by the utter incapacity of the ignorant inhabitants to manage anything for themselves that calls for more than a very low degree of intelligence. Lest, however, it might be urged that government ownership and supervision is likely to lead to failure, the actual results attained in India may be very properly here cited. During recent years, the British government has spent about seventy millions of dollars, in irrigating works, and others are in progress of construction which will require half as much more to complete them. In almost every instance, the investment has been profitable, and in some cases enormously so, both in the way of water rent, and in service to the cultivators of the soil. The total annual revenue to the government from the works is more than five millions of dollars, or seven and three-fourths per cent on the cost."

And so it is that national, state and municipal governments of our own country are brought face to face with a system of irrigation so easy of realization, as to only require the application of laws everywhere governing in nature, giving them an opportunity to work out for themselves results at once universal, all pervading and endless in cycles of beneficence. While Great Britain is engaged in India not only in the construction of reservoirs for the storage of the waters of springs and streams, but for gathering in the rains and dews for purposes of irrigation, spending millions annually in creation of works for that purpose, and other millions in keeping them in repair, our own country, possessing a domain of vaster extent than that of any nation of the world and of incomparably greater value, has only to enter upon her own possessions, and by trenching her mountain sides beget reservoirs as enduring as the foundations of earth. Let no one doubt that the alkaline deposits in the Great Desert lands will be removed from the soil by this running of the waters through them, leaving only such proportions of alkali as is required for the best developement of plant growth.

But whence will come the money with which to do this work is the question. Our answer is, let such policies be pursued by governments, state and national, as will encourage and foster industries. Let the world find out that intoxicating liquors used as a beverage are a curse, and provide for the suppression of their sale as such. This will save thousands of millions of money and countless numbers of lives annually. Let our schools and churches, Sunday schools and educational institutions and agencies generally, frown upon, discourage, and ultimately prohibit the production and use of tobacco, a greater curse, if possible, than rum. Let no party as such, attempt these reforms, but let the work be done by men and women everywhere, irrespective of party or sect. Last, not least, let pure water be everywhere sought, and let the waters be nowhere wasted, but made to do their perfect work everywhere.

CHAPTER VII.

THE EXPENSE OF THE NEW SYSTEM.

"It costs five hundred dollars to fit a single acre under Cole's system," exclaims an occasional critic. "What farmer can afford such an outlay?"

"Not one in a thousand, probably not one in ten thousand," is our own answer.

Never have we suggested such cost for farm lands. So far as we are personally concerned, we have nearly finished work on five acres, having in view the utmost possibilities of production in horticulture. No plat of land equaling our five acres can be found on the face of the earth. Were it within an hour's run by rail of any of our larger cities, this plat would be worth more money than any equal area not under glass in the world. It would be worth more than any greenhouse, costing from ten to twenty times as much. In the mere *fitting of this land*, the cost has not exceeded $1,500. Here are the figures, moneys expended for all purposes, sober facts that do not lie:

Expenses for 1882, not exceeding $300; for 1883, about $500; for 1884, not exceeding $800. This has been my investment up to April 1st, 1885. I have this season expended about $700 up to this this date August 13, 1885. Thus twenty-three hundred dollars has fitted my land, *planted it to trees and plants, cared for and harvested and marketed all products, paid for manures etc., and during that period has returned at least $500 in excess of expenses.*

Over and again have we endeavored to undeceive the public in regard to this matter of cost, but in vain. Barely one agricultural paper in the land has sought to aid us in this; all others, so far as we are aware, have striven to increase the extent of the false estimate. The *Husbandman*, however, published at Elmira, N. Y., has not only treated us fairly, but generously. As this great paper is an organ of the Grange, and the medium through which the famed farmers of the Chemung Valley make themselves heard, its voice is potential.

Mr. James McCann, President, and Mr. George W. Hoffman, ex-President of the Farmers' Club of Elmira, together with Mr. W. A. Armstrong, the latter having no superior among agricultural editors of our State, have reputations quite as great as those possessed by most of the eminent men of the agricultural press. These have carefully examined "The New Agriculture," and will vouch for the fact that we have never advised expending more than from thirty to fifty dollars an acre on farm lands; yet we propose to fit fifty acres at a cost not to exceed one hundred and fifty dollars per acre. Thus fitted, our lands for agricultural and horticultural purposes combined, will doubtless return good profits on an outlay of from three to five hundred dollars per acre for the full fifty acres.

My five acres will return when in full bearing, at least five hundred dollars to an acre in home markets. The remaining forty-five acres in farm crops will without doubt average fifty, possibly an hundred dollars an acre net annually. I leave the reader to make his own figures and decide whether it will pay. The conclusion thus far reached by myself, having tried "The New Agriculture," is, that no business pays as well as farming and gardening, under systems of subsurface, subterranean or underground-irrigation.

SINGLE TOMATO PLANT.

The following communications addressed respectively to us and to the Editor of *The Farm Journal*, of Philadelphia, by a farmer who has adopted our system, is evidence of the fact that one hundred dollars per acre will cover the cost of fitting lands under "The New Agriculture," for *horticultural* purposes.

MAINSBURG, PA., Sept. 21, 1885.

Hon. A. N. Cole,

DEAR SIR :—I find in the *Farm Journal* for September, edited by Mr. W. Atkinson, of Philadelphia, the following mention :

"Mr. Cole's new agriculture is not likely to be extensively imitated. It cost him $500 an acre to make the stone ditches, and yet, he has it patented."

I am satisfied this criticism by Mr. A. is to be ascribed to his want of knowledge upon the subject. If he can be undeceived, and enlisted in favor of your system, he would prove a powerful ally. I enclose a letter which I have written him, and if you approve it, I will request its publication.

I finished my little model farm a week ago, and have set a few rows of strawberries, which are looking finely. It has been fitted to the letter in obedience to your directions—first, well rotted manure plowed in; next well rotted manure and leached ashes dragged in; then two inches thick of fine washings from barnyard, where it had lodged on upper portion of the garden. The mulching with leaves will be attended to at proper time, and any other suggestions you may make will be gladly adopted.

Leading from the barn which is eighty feet long is an underdrain which carries off quite an amount of water during rains. The surface water from the side hill, and water from the eavetroughs, together with that from the drain under the wall of the barn, is gathered in to prevent washing through the barnyard. This additional supply is connected through an underdrain into the trenches.

I do not see why the longing for perfection which is presumed to be natural to most minds, is not satisfied by your system, nor do I see why you may not now say, "what more can I do in my vineyard, that has not been done in it?"

Yours Respectfully.
E. R. Maine.

In explanation of the above our readers need hardly be told that its author is one of several who began work under our system. Mr. Maine has done his work in a way to insure success. His thoroughness in the matter of manuring, will secure returns the ensuing year. Had he manured less at the outset, it would have required a year or two longer to show the effects of the system, but time has been gained and that is an important consideration.

The following communication was addressed by Mr. Maine to the Editor of *The Farm Journal* :

Mainsburg, Pa., Sept., 21, 1885.

Mr. W. Atkinson,

Dear Sir :—Having seen the working model of Mr. Cole's new system of irrigation at Wellsville, Allegany County, N. Y., I was so favorably impressed as to induce me to fit a small piece of land, intending fully and fairly to test its merits. So far I can only report upon the cost.

To fit an acre as I have done for horticulture, takes eighty rods of trench, and sixteen rods for drain. I enclose diagram of one acre, 8 x 20 rods. First trench lengthwise one rod from side of the plat; the next, two rods below the first, making in all four trenches twenty rods long, and two rods apart. The cross drains are eight rods apart in the middle, and four rods from the ends.

The maximum cost for digging the trenches in any soil, $3\frac{1}{2}$ ft. deep and 2 ft. wide is 75 cents per rod, and the cross drains 35 cents, making $65.60 per acre. (See diagram on following page.)

It will be safe to say that the entire cost of labor will be less than one hundred dollars per acre. In this section the stone for filling in are of no value, and the work of filling is comparatively light.

As a farmer, and interested personally like yourself, I write this more especially that *The Farm Journal* may not occupy a false position inadvertently. If one half of what the system appears to be is true, it is the biggest thing that was ever thought of since the world was made. If land can be made to produce all it is capable of doing by an equable supply of moisture and the element of uncertainty removed in farming, the cost of preparing the land would be small, compared to the benefits received. *If the cost is all, Mr. Cole's system is an assured success and it will win its way whether favored or opposed by the press.*

	TWENTY RODS.	
	First trench.	
EIGHT RODS	Second trench.	
	Third trench.	
	Fourth trench.	
Cross drains.		Cross drains.

In fairness, we should, it seems to me, withold an opinion, while awaiting developments, and if there is anything likely to interpose in favor of the farmer, in Heaven's name let us not oppose it.

If you can consistently publish the statement herein made, it would, I feel, tend to correct a prevalent error, and would be esteemed a favor by your friend and well wisher,

E. R. MAINE.

Though several doubters have not omitted to say that our system is one calling for expenditures causing the average farmer, should he adopt it, to start back in fear of bankruptcy, we have in no instance controverted their statements, preferring to appeal to the public through the medium of our book. We now say, once for all, that the fitting of lands from year to year with the plow and the spade, and their fertilization by methods hitherto in vogue, are waste and extravagance by the side of those called for in "The New Agriculture."

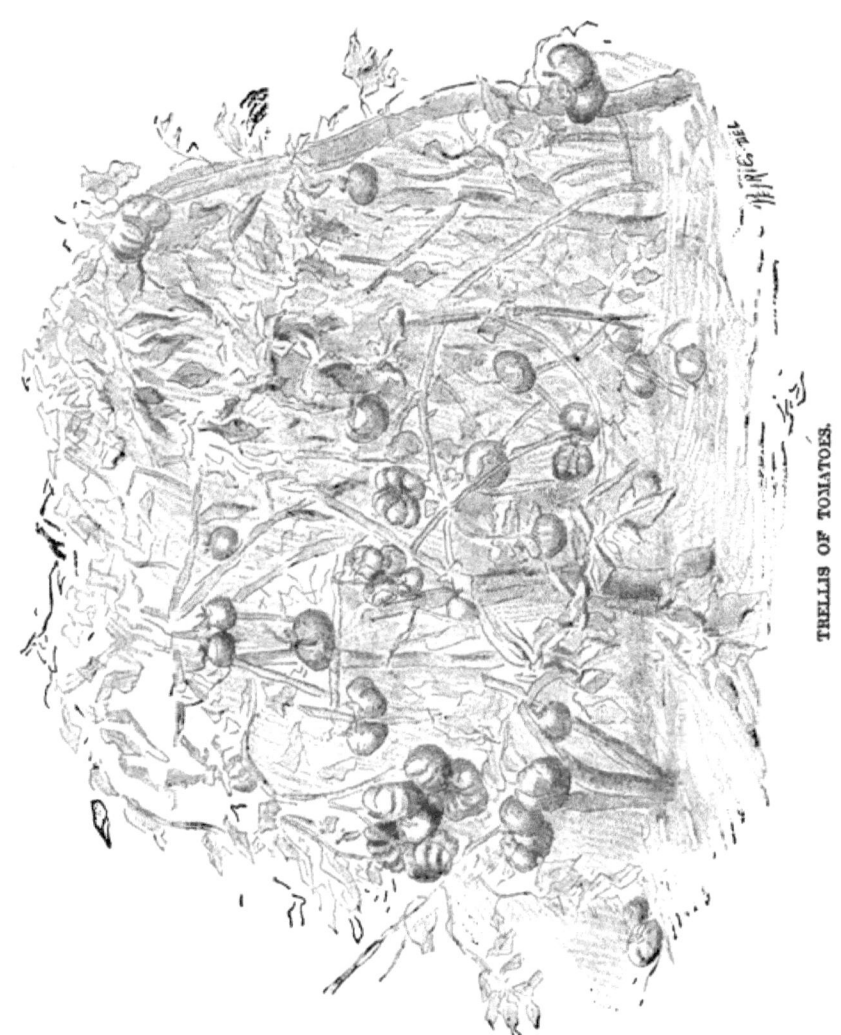

TRELLIS OF TOMATOES.

CHAPTER VIII.

1850—1885-"THE HOME ON THE HILLSIDE" THEN AND NOW.

Mr. William Pooler, one of our present neighbors, built in 1853 and resided in the house now known as "The Home on the Hillside." He forwards us the following communication.

"I think it was about 1850, that I purchased the place on which you now live. Wellsville was then in the woods, and the Erie road had been built through from New York to Dunkirk. I had been familiar with hardpan lands in Chenango and other counties of the Southern Tier, and had done something of subsoiling in more ways than one, and had become convinced that Allegany hardpan had only to be properly treated, and it could be made rich and productive. My hillside had been cleared for several years being one of the earliest lots improved in what is now Wellsville, then the town of Scio.

"There was an old orchard on the place, and also a tree which I shall never forget. It was not in the orchard but stood by itself, a little to the northwest of the house, and was a Roxbury russet; no more worthless fruit could have been anywhere found. Yesterday (Sept. 22, 1885) I plucked from this tree two apples; one the smallest I could find, the other of average size of those with which the tree was so loaded as to bow its branches to the ground upon which the lower limbs rested. I should judge there were twenty-five bushels of apples on this tree two thirds grown.

These apples on the first of October in the years 1853, '54 and '55 did not average larger than crab apples at that time of year. They were not so large at harvesting as the small one I picked yesterday, nor were they quarter as large as most of the apples on the tree at this time. The tree was then about ten years old, and was covered with moss and in all respects of no value, and I threatened at the time to cut it down as a cumberer of the ground. I should guess that the tree might possibly have borne two bushels of apples in a bearing year, and we did not pretend to gather them. The apples now on the tree are large, fine and fair; in fact, they are the finest russets I ever saw.

"You showed me Early Rose potatoes grown this year, the like of which I never saw anywhere. Some of these weighed from a pound to a pound and a half apiece, and I should think one would weigh two pounds. You assured me that you had grown them at the rate of over one thousand bushels to the acre the present season, and I have no reason to doubt it. As there is no fungus on your grounds, there is no rot. The tomatoes all over the town are rotting, but I did not observe any rotten ones on your place, and I certainly never saw such splendid fruit, nor anything like as many to the plant.

"I gave you an account of my experiment with two acres of potatoes in 1854, and here repeat it. The plot on which I planted is a portion of the ground now embraced in your garden, on which this year has been grown such crops as I never set eyes on before. I fitted these two acres with greater care and painstaking than any equal amount of ground in my life, mixing a portion of the subsoil with that of the surface, and covered it deep with well rotted barnyard manure, making it very rich. A careful man and a good farmer planted the two acres to potatoes on halves, and I realized just thirty bushels for my half. This completely discouraged me and though there was then no better house in Wellsville than the one I had built upon the place, and the barn was nearly new, I gave up and sold the property for what I could get. You told me yesterday that you valued your two acres completed at $5,000 an acre, and that it was paying well at that. As five thousand dollars at six per cent. interest only gives $300, I do not wonder, since I am sure you are getting two or three times that from an acre. I have seen the strawberries and other fruits and vegetables as sold in this market for the last three or four years and have eaten of the fruit, and have never seen anything anywhere near as large, beautiful and fine flavored.

"You yesterday showed me pods of peas, and I carried home specimens with eight peas in a pod, of such marvelous size, as to astonish me. The peas were of the dwarf variety, as shown by the vines, and yet they were as large as Delaware grapes. You assured me you grew five hundred bushels of pods to the acre of these peas, and I believe you, since your Champions of England, on vines higher than any man's head, loaded with pods and still covered with blossoms, presented such a sight as I never saw before. Your squashes, beets, cabbage and cauliflower were all very fine, and as for the squashes, I never saw anything in my life so astonishing. Though quinces are rarely grown in Allegany County, I saw as fine ones as I ever came across anywhere.

"Nothing so much surprised me as the change wrought in the soil. The cold clay and hardpan had been turned into a soil, deep, soft and very rich, growing all forms of plants, bushes and trees to perfection. You say your system wipes out the hardpan, and it certainly does.

"This latter feature of your plan surprised me more than any other, but perhaps I should except from this your spring brook, and that stream of pure cold water, flowing out from the pipe in the rear of the house, there being no springs on this part of the place. Nobody can look down into your trenches where open, and see the long stretches of spring water in them as I did, and not discover that you save all the water which falls upon the hillside, using what is needed for the growing crop and the remainder, by far the greater portion, running off in purity. Though before my visit of yesterday, I was convinced your system was a success, I left your place prepared to say what I now do.

"Your discovery has no equal, nor do I believe anything will hereafter be discovered so important to the health and prosperity of the people.

WILLIAM POOLER.

Mr. Pooler's statement is one in accord with the testimony of everyone who has looked over our place, and yet his evidence is most convincing from the fact that he personally tried the experiment of making farming an object on the land we now possess, and though doing his utmost at a time when the demand for farm products in home markets exceeded the supply, failed to make farming a success, owing to the paucity and poverty of the producing soil.

Let us now, in turn, post the books :

We have grown the present year Early Rose potatoes without rot, larger, finer and better than any we have ever seen in our entire life, at the rate, at least, of twelve hundred bushels to the acre.

We have grown strawberries of extraordinary size and flavor at the rate of three to four hundred bushels per acre.

We have grown raspberries five hundred bushels per acre.

We have become convinced, from experiments made already, that next year we will be enabled to grow blackberries exceeding in quantity to the acre the growth of our raspberries.

We have grown a few clusters of grapes on newly set vines to

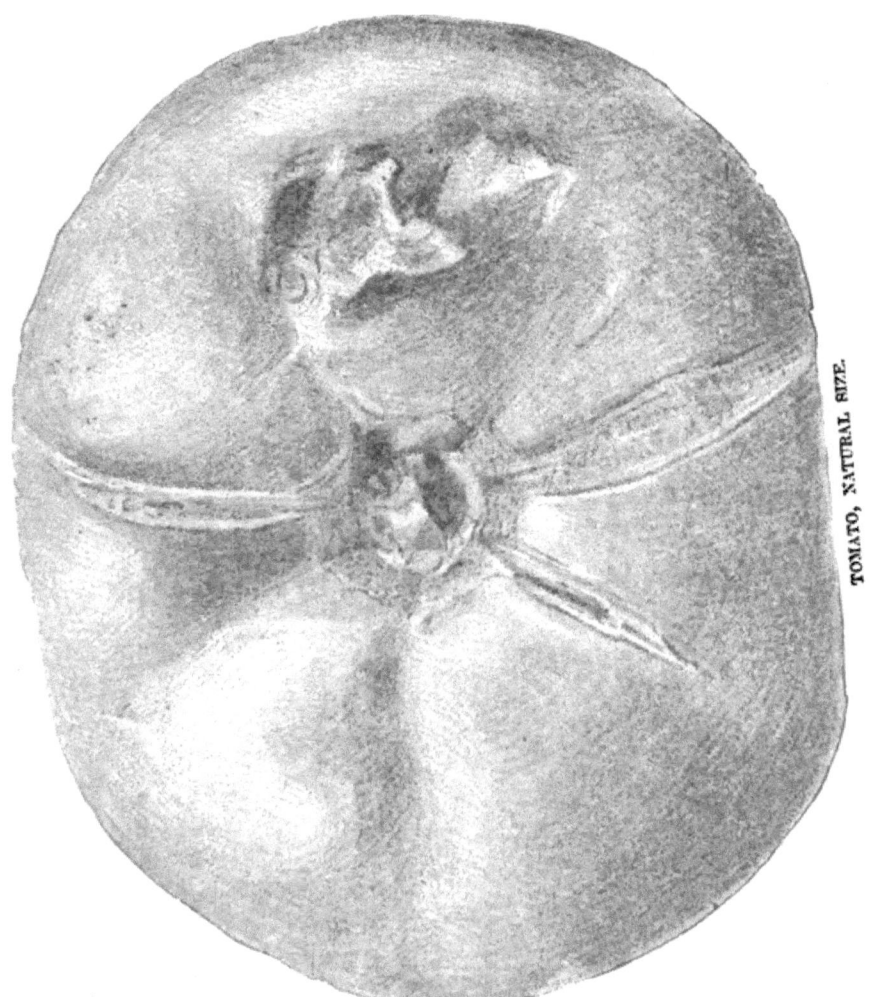

TOMATO, NATURAL SIZE.

such size, beauty and perfection, as to convince us that five pounds of superior quality can be grown under our system where one can be produced under established methods.

We have grown marrow fat peas to nearly or quite double the size of the ordinary product at the rate of upwards of five hundred bushels of pods to the acre; we have also grown an equal number of bushels to the acre of pods of McLean's dwarf varieties and have now growing, a drill of the Champions of England, loaded with pods promising upwards of a thousand bushels per acre, at least.

We have grown the ordinary blood beet to a length of three and a half feet, and become convinced that these may be more than doubled in length under the best conditions of our system.

We have brought out from our hillside a flowing well of crystal waters of a degree of purity and temperature to grow brook trout.

We are convinced, that what we have done in the growth of the fruits of the earth can be done in all regions of hills, valleys and undulations, and that too, at a cost in fitting farm lands, of no more than fifty dollars per acre, and, in a majority of instances, not exceeding thirty dollars.

We are convinced that models as perfect as our own can be prepared at an expense of no more than two hundred dollars per acre, and in a majority of instances they will cost no more than one hundred dollars per acre.

Of the fruits pictured along the pages of our book, we will only say that the quince, measuring twelve inches in circumference is no more than three-fourths grown. We grew specimens in 1882 to the circumference of fifteen inches, the size of a pint bowl. That the specimen protographed would in a month longer have grown to a circumference of fifteen inches, we are well convinced.

The largest specimen of the Lombard plum, a drawing of which is given, is somewhat less than another stolen from the tree before fully ripe. None of the pictures of the plums come up to the reality, since we were obliged to pluck them before fully ripe, to save them from being stolen.

During a visit to our home by Mr. William C. Harris, on September 17, we plucked a head of early Paris cauliflower, which had grown in twelve days to the circumference of thirty-one inches. This was measured in the presence of Mrs. Harris. At same date, we dug one hill of Early Rose potatoes, the vines by no means dead, but the tubers still growing, which were weighed by Messrs W. C. Harris, and J. H. Selkreg, with results as follows:

The potatoes from this one hill weighed $16\frac{1}{2}$ pounds, upwards of a peck to the hill. Five of the potatoes measured the largest way round as follows: 17, $17\frac{1}{2}$, 18, 18, and $18\frac{1}{2}$ inches, and all averaged nine inches in girth. The memorandum from which we copy is in the handwriting of Senator Selkreg, and signed by him. That the potatoes from this one hill would have weighed twenty pounds, had they been left to their full growth, we have little doubt.

We conclude this chapter by a statement, made as follows by E. F. Stelle, an intelligent farmer, who has been the superintendent during the last two seasons of our model five acres.

"To all whom it may concern.

"A year ago the 29th of June last, I called on Mr. Cole having in view work on his place as a temporary expedient, not having the least idea of continuing in his employment more than a week or two at the utmost. I considered myself a good farmer, and felt that I knew considerable about gardening. I had heard incidentally of a new system of agriculture and horticulture of which Mr. Cole was the discoverer. This he explained briefly, but at the same time in a way which seemed rather to discourage than encourage me to look into it. I saw clearly that the author of "The New Agriculture" took every man who came to ask him questions, as coming more from curiosity to see what he would say, than to obtain information. The more Mr. Cole said, the deeper became my interest in his conversation, since I saw at a glance the man was talking of a subject on which he was well posted.

"Looking me over, he concluded I was hardly stout enough to work in his trenches, but after some hesitation engaged me to work for a few days setting strawberry plants. He gave directions that no plant should be set till every stone, big or little, lying in reach of the roots was removed, giving as a reason, that if the root struck a stone, it would be attacked by fungus, and that the plant would languish, if not die, and would bear little or no fruit. He pointed out plants having a sickly appearance, and directed me to pull them up, dig down for the cause of unthrift, and removing it, set a new and healthy one in its place.

"I soon found an abundance of work, since fully one-third of his plants, set by careless or inexperienced laborers, gave evidence of fungus at their roots. Security from fungus, seemed to me at first a large part of Mr. Cole's system.

"'Give your plants plenty of water, removing obstructions, so that the roots will not strike them,' he said, 'and there will be no fungus, unless it is planted in the soil by decaying wood or uncomposted and fermenting manures, or by water-logged lands.'

"I saw at a glance that Mr. Cole's system removed difficulties, giving his plants an opportunity of eating and drinking all they wanted, making their own selection. I had not been a month at work before becoming more deeply interested in Mr. Cole's methods of cultivating the soil, than in anything I had ever worked at. While I worked for wages, I worked also to get knowledge, and though approaching three score years and ten, I have become a deeply interested student of a system, bound, I am satisfied, to become general throughout the land.

"Always taking a deep interest in orcharding, I have taken particular notice of the effect of Mr. Cole's system on apple-trees. I have seen an old tree made to cast off its dead bark, and drop its mosses, the trunk and limbs to the end of every twig having a bright and vigorous growth. The old apple tree standing alone on the trenched portion of Mr. Cole's farm has been with me an object of continual interest. Mr. Cole has had this tree photographed, the picture being taken several days ago. Even then, the lower limbs had in some instances reached the ground, and were resting upon it. Other limbs are following suit, and it looks now as though all of the lower limbs would rest upon the ground. I have urged Mr. Cole to have the tree propped up, but he insists upon it that none of the limbs having broken, none will. Mr. Cole tells me the top of the tree has nearly doubled in spread since trenching above it, and this I cannot doubt, as it has grown since I began working for him as I never saw any tree grow before. I have rarely seen a tree so bright in the lustre of its bark throughout its entire top, and to the end of every twig. The old and shaggy bark on the body has been continually dropping off, moss disappearing, and the tree throughout has the appearance of youth, and yet, according to Mr. Pooler, who knew it as a ten year old tree, thirty years ago, it should have reached its prime. That it has grown nearly as much in three years past, as in its entire life before, I am satisfied. The fruit on this tree, Mr. Pooler says, grew no larger than a good sized thorn apple, when he owned the place, and was an insignificant and worthless russet. The apple as seen at present, shows so little of the russet coating, as to have the appearance of a greening, when seen at a little distance; hence the

APPLE, NATURAL SIZE, AS GROWN IN 1855 ON OLD APPLE TREE.

APPLE, NATURAL SIZE, AS GROWN IN 1885 ON OLD APPLE TREE.

statements getting into the papers that Mr. Cole had turned a russet apple into a greening, nor do I wonder at it since I must say the apples resemble greenings. To describe this tree is impossible. I have never seen such a wonder, bearing such fine fruit, tender and juicy, and of matchless flavor. I think there is nearly twenty bushels of apples on the tree, were they gathered to-day, and whether to place the estimate at thirty or forty at harvest time, I am at a loss, since the fruit swells out so from day to day as to bewilder me.

"Still more remarkable is the effect upon another tree which I will endeavor to describe. Mr. Cole took one of his men a few days after his great show on the 7th of July, and going into his orchard, picked out two trees well loaded with fruit. One was young, eight years old. Mr. Cole tells me it was a Flemish beauty; the other was an old tree. I should think it one of the oldest trees of a very old orchard, there being no older orchard, as I am told, in town. The ground was cultivated as a garden about the young tree, while the old one stood in the sod of years. About both trees trenches were dug and finished under Mr. Cole's system. Overflows were provided, and the ground broken and well manured. The apples on the Flemish beauty were nearly half grown, and by the first of September presented an appearance in marked contrast with those on other early trees around it. The fruit grew rapidly, matured early, and if finer fruit was ever produced, I never saw it. It is the old tree, however, bearing a nameless apple, that presents at this time a wonderful transformation. The apples were about the size of thorn plums when the tree was trenched around. Mr. Cole tells me that while the fruit growing on this tree is not the Lady apple, he, three years ago, gave them to his grand-children as such. He also tells me that an ounce was the average weight of the apple three years ago. There are now apples growing on the tree of three ounces weight, and the growth continues at a rapid rate. Where they will stop nobody knows. That apples will be gathered at harvest weighing five or six ounces, I believe. Their luster is astonishing. In fact, I have never seen their equal. The fruit developing to-day, is incomparably finer than any on the place.

"Suffice it to say, that results thus far realized by Mr. Cole in orcharding, justifies the following copied from the *Husbandman* at the conclusion of his address before the Farmer's Club at Elmira a month ago.

"'I conclude my remarks by saying that from the very first I have found the increase in size, beauty and perfection of fruits of all kinds simply incredible. I am this season making experiments on two apple trees, one set four years ago, two or three years old when set, and the other a tree at least forty years old, selected from others in our orchard, and judging from present appearance of these trees, the farmer who allows five years to pass over his head without trenching his orchard, should give up farming altogether.''

"While on this subject I cannot omit saying that being a Jerseyman by birth and bringing up, I have from boyhood taken a deep interest in everything connected with fruit raising and market gardening. I have seen more manure used annually on one acre in New Jersey than Mr. Cole has used on his whole five acres during the last two seasons, and in no instance have I known more than a quarter of a crop grown in New Jersey or in Western Pennsylvania (where I now reside and own a small farm under a good state of cultivation) when compared with crops grown by Mr. Cole. From the first day of my superintendence of the "Home on the Hillside" I have made a study of fungoid growths, the seeds of fungus, their attack upon roots, and effects generally upon plants, and I am prepared to say that after reading works on agriculture and horticulture for fifty years, the agricultural and horticultural journals of the country as they have come in my way, I confess to have learned more since taking charge of Mr. Cole's model five acres than during all the former years of my life. I am convinced that the seeds of fungus are engendered under many other conditions than those described in the following extract from Bulletin No. 2 of the New Series treating of pear blight at the State Experimental Station at Geneva.

"'The disease is due to living germs. These germs can multiply indefinitely in any damp spot where there is decomposing vegetable matter. From such places they are raised into the air when dry or carried up by moisture. From the air they lodge upon the trees, and when the conditions are favorable pass into the tissues and cause blight. The conditions referred to are in general (1) very tender tissues, such as are found within the flowers and at the ends of expanding shoots in spring, and (2) a moist atmosphere. No varieties are entirely blight proof, but the disease spreads so slowly in some that they receive little injury, especially when not making too rapid growth. The reason why the blight, when seen in July and later, does not pass directly from one limb to another, or from one tree to another, is because in the first place the germs cannot escape, being confined by the bark, or else escape in a viscid exudation which holds them firmly together, and in the second place there are very few places on the tree at this time of the year where the surface tissues are sufficiently tender for them to find an entrance.'"

"Certainly the disease is due to living germs, nor is this all; for in the air above, in the earth beneath, and in waters on and under the earth are the seeds of death arising from decomposition and from the stagnation of the waters, That these can everywhere be kept in motion, regulated in their flow and kept at nearly uniform temperature summer and winter, cannot be longer questioned, for Mr. Cole has demonstrated the fact. He runs the rain water through his 'retorts,' as he calls his trenches, and it is perfectly filtered. He has this season experimented on water drawn from the main of the Wellsville waterworks, and that too in the midst of a drought so severe as to dry up the springs feeding the reservoir, causing the water remaining in it to stagnate, rendering it unfit for use. He has purified this water completely.

"What Mr. Cole does by way of purifying the water falling from the clouds, I can perhaps best illustrate by the fact that a year ago last fall, (the autumn before my employment by him), he corded up for composting, thirty or forty wagon loads of manure in a winrow about twelve rods long near the summit of his hillside. After I commenced work for him in the spring of last year, when it rained the water would issue from this winrow of the color of lye and running into the first trench below, this liquid manure water would become perfectly filtered, and flow out as pure as the purest spring water. This convinced me that a single trench sunk below a barnyard would save the manure otherwise lost by the wash of rains and melting snows; and that trenching below stables, sties, hen-houses, and above, below, round and about dwellings and outhouses, and dropping the waters deep down, by overflow from trench to trench and by movement through the surface soil, and percolation through the subsoil, the ground would absorb all impurities. I have become satisfied that the stagnant waters of swamps and ponds, and those from drains and sewers can be dropped into trenches and filtered perfectly and made as pure as the purest spring water. This demonstrates the fact that by the use of Mr. Cole's system an end would come to pear blight, rot in potatoes, of tomatoes, and of rot and premature decay of all kinds. This very season he has been digging Early Rose potatoes of a size and beauty never equalled in the experience of any one who has seen them; the vines continued growing for weeks after all others were dead in fields round about, not treated as Mr. Cole is treating his lands. His potatoes average from three to five times the weight of those grown under old methods, and that he has this season grown from ten to twelve hundred bushels to an acre, is a fact, and I have not seen a rotten potato on his place inside of his lines of trenching, while they are found thick enough, on that portion not trenched.

"What is true of potatoes, is equally true of tomatoes. Where very little manure has been applied directly to the soil, and the waters have been run beneath the plants, impregnated with the manure from the winrow above, not a rotten potato has this year been found on any portion of the place except where chip manure was used.

"I need not say any more on this point. If there is a person in the world who doubts, they should come and see the squashes growing now on this place. At this date, the last days of September, the largest of these squashes, a Chili specimen, measures fifty by fifty-four inches around, and will weigh upwards of an hundred pounds, and seems growing at a rate of three or four pounds per day, and that it will reach and pass the size and weight of the famous specimen of the same variety seen a year or two ago at the seed store of Mr. Peter Henderson in New York, is not unreasonable. This of course depends upon the frost holding back. That this squash would, under conditions of underground irrigation, reach a weight of three hundred pounds in New Jersey, on Long Island, Staten Island, or in Southern Pennsylvania, I have no doubt. What it would do farther south must be left for experiment. Should the Government conclude to establish an Experimental Station at Washington, as has been suggested, it is not improbable that specimens of the Chili squash will be grown weighing from four to five hundred pounds.

"Most remarkable of all, however, are two specimens of the yellow cheese pumpkin. These vary but little in size, having already grown to a girth of four feet and eight inches, and increasing at the rate of an inch a day. At no time has the growth seemed more rapid. The rapidity of growth increases flavor and tenderness of all vegetables and fruits. The blood beet has this year been grown to the length of three feet by Mr. Cole, and that a foot more will be added this season, seems probable. That they can be grown to a much greater length by preparing a soil deep enough, with water beneath, I am quite sure.

"Mr. Cole, not having protected his quince trees from the depredations of the borer, his quinces are not as large at this time of year, so he tells me, as those grown by him five years ago in his first test of his system. That he then grew specimens to the size of a pint bowl, his family and neighbors bear witness. The specimen he has just had photographed measures at this time nine inches in circumference, and as seen at Rider's photograph gallery in Wellsville, N. Y., exhibited in his glass case is mistaken for wax-work. That this quince would have grown to a girth of from one foot to one foot and three inches, had it been left to full development, I am quite sure. E. F. STELLE.

WELLSVILLE, N. Y. Sept. 25, 1885.

"To all whom it may concern.

"This will certify that I met Mr. Stelle the fore part of the present week, while looking over the place I once owned and abandoned because I could not make a living upon it on account of the poverty of the soil, and his statement having been submitted to me, I declare it a fair and truthful one from beginning to end, corresponding with observations made by myself set forth in my own statement, made three days since." WILLIAM POOLER.

WELLSVILLE, Sept. 26, 1885.

CHAPTER IX.

MANURING UNDER THE NEW SYSTEM—THE AMERICAN POMOLOGICAL SOCIETY—
A WELCOME FOR ALL AT THE "HOME ON THE HILLSIDE."

As the success of our system has been mainly attributed, by several doubters, to our methods of fertilizing, we desire to put on record that our practice is simply that of slight top dressing, with compost applied in the early spring; the land having been first prepared as described in Chapter VII by Mr. Maine. We have no hesitation in saying that not to exceed one-fourth of the quantity of manure is necessary under the methods of the new as compared with those of the old agriculture.

At the conclusion of an address made by us on Aug. 29, 1885, before the Farmers Club of Elmira, the Hon. John H. Selkreg, who had recently visited our hillside in company with Professor Roberts of Cornell, was called upon for his views of "The New Agriculture." His response was reported in the *Husbandman*, of Elmira, N. Y., as follows:

"I might with a good deal of propriety, enter most earnest protest against Mr. Cole's coaching you to call on me for testimony that is not needed. The position is by no means pleasant, because I have not expected to add anything to what has been said, nor am I in a very high degree capable of judging questions with which you, as farmers, are far more familiar.

"I came to your city on business which occupied time, so that the train which I expected to take had gone before I was ready, and I at once resolved to come here, because I desired to hear about the New Agriculture, and to see friends, particularly Mr. Cole, with whom I might claim slight relation, dating back to its origin somewhere near Adam. I am not a farmer by a long way, yet I appreciate the wisdom in the adage that glorifies a man who makes two blades of grass grow where but one grew before. I believe in improvement, and particularly in the most important industry of the land—agriculture. There is great need of every improvement, for farmers have too long clung to old methods. There is neither use nor sense in farmers staying by the old methods employed by their fathers a hundred years ago, for conditions have changed, and there is, therefore, imperative necessity that better means be employed—improved methods, every advancement that will lead to larger returns, and increase of profits.

"This, it is true, may be regarded as theory. It is theory. Yet it is good common sense. I know very little about practical farming, for my experience is confined mainly to a garden of about forty feet square, and I am bound to say that I do not care for that in the best way, as anybody who inspects the work would be sure to say. I had heard a great deal about the New Agriculture before curiosity was greatly excited, but at last I began to wonder, —can these things be true as reported? Is it possible that Mr. Cole is forcing earth to production far greater than under previous conditions? I visited his grounds, saw his trenches, examined his work and its results; but all this was necessary before I could believe that what appeared like extravagant claims were based in truth. I found they were. I found that he had made most wonderful improvement in land that in the outset was poor. I saw him but a few days ago dig potatoes, nearly a peck from a single hill. I saw on the 7th of July on his grounds strawberries mar-

QUINCE, NATURAL SIZE.

velous in size and delicious in flavor. Last Tuesday I picked peapods of a dwarf variety, the pods five inches in length and each containing eight large peas—the products of his improved land. Now, when I find these evidences of improvement I must say there is really something worth considering in the system by which the gain is made. That the crops are improved may be determined easily by comparison with similar products on other lands adjoining that which Mr. Cole has treated. Nothing of the kind can be found. No strawberries of large size, or even of ordinary size, were possible on the unimproved grounds near Mr. Cole last July; no potatoes of large yield, no peas of large growth. Mr. Cole's lands alone have these remarkable products. Then they are convincing evidence of merit in his treatment, whatever that may be.

"I do not know that all his claims will be sustained,—that he will realize all he expects. But I do know that he has effected wonderful improvement in his lands, and I believe that similar improvement, perhaps less in degree, may be made in the soils of these uplands in all the hilly lands of Steuben, Allegany, Chemung, Tioga, Tompkins, and many other counties where conditions are similar. It is something to be proud of, to take unproductive apple trees and by treatment of the soil make them bear fruit of fine character, and this is what Mr. Cole has done, the fruit being far superior to that on other trees but a little way off; yet the trees were formerly under the same conditions. So in tomato plants. Will I seem to be extravagant in statement when I say that a single vine on Mr. Cole's improved land has thirty or forty pounds of tomatoes?"

Mr. Cole. From one to one and a half bushels.

Senator Selkreg. No doubt; the yield is simply marvelous. It is difficult to comprehend the change effected in all the products of that improved land. The lessons there spread out to view are worthy of your careful consideration. They may not be decisive of all matters suggested, nor even conclusive in any matter, except that the system employed tends to wonderful improvement of products. There may be ways of cheapening the work. All these matters are for your consideration.

W. A. ARMSTRONG. It is alleged that Mr. Cole has used a great deal of manure on his grounds, and that the remarkable fruits of which he speaks may be credited properly to that source. Now it will be gratifying to gentlemen here to learn just how much manure has been used, in order that credit may be given where it belongs.

MR. COLE. In 1883 I used possibly sixty loads of manure on the whole five acres under treatment—not more than sixty loads of barnyard manure, composted with muck and all the forest leaves I could get, with some lime and some ashes, all used on the surface. That is the extent of the application, and no manure has been applied since. I say sixty loads, because I wish to exceed the amount; I am sure that not more than that quantity was applied, but I have not the exact figures, and am, therefore, obliged to fix an outside limit which is entirely safe. I believe this land, after three years more, will want no more manure, for enough will be obtained through the solids left by waters, which in draining away, part with all substances, animalculæ and everything else that in its decay will furnish plant food. You will observe that everything the water contains must stop in the soil and be held for use, and there is enough in insect life, if it can be appropriated, to nourish plants quite as effectually as moderate application of manure. This very morning I gave one of my men fifty cents to buy Paris green to kill potato beetles on the vines, without a doubt that the beetles, when incorporated in the soil, will be worth more than the money and the labor of destroying them in the fertilizing influence they will have on the soil.

Three years ago, I prepared a bed for asparagus and put in chip manure, a liberal supply, some of it pine chips, that remain there still without going to decay as rapidly as I desired. Where that chip manure is used, there is fungoid growth. A few tomato vines planted along the border yield fruit that has rotted, the trouble caused by chip manure. There is no other place on my grounds where rot affects tomatoes, and in this spot the trouble is clearly traceable to chip manure.

W. A. ARMSTRONG. The answer to my question is not entirely satisfactory, because with the sixty loads of manure there is all the leaf mould that Mr. Cole could gather. Now, if we had a safe estimate of that, the whole matter would be clear.

MR. COLE. I can only say that I have gathered all the leaves from forest and other places that I could conveniently get, but the whole has not been much. I cannot state the exact amount.

G. W. HOFFMAN. The sixty loads of manure mean the compost in which the leaves were incorporated?

MR. COLE. Yes; and that is the limit. Sixty loads covers everything.

G. W. HOFFMAN. We have here a tobacco farmer, who knows very well the amount required on good lands to secure a full growth of tobacco—Mr. Chamberlain, whose experience is extended.

GEORGE CHAMBERLAIN. I use twenty loads of manure to the acre the first year; after that about ten loads each year, provided I can get so much.

G. W. HOFFMAN. And a load is a cord and a half or more?

GEORGE CHAMBERLAIN. Two cords.

G. W. HOFFMAN. Then there are forty cords used on an acre, and in the next year, if tobacco is continued, twenty cords—the amount in either case much greater than Mr. Cole has used in the three years. I visited his place July 7th, and saw most wonderful growth of plants and fruits, particularly strawberries, while alongside the lands he has treated every kind of plant growth was stunted. He has certainly proved great possibilities in production on lands that at the beginning were very poor.

Mr. Cole. I wish to call again on Senator Selkreg, who has examined my grounds lately. I want to ask him if he saw any appearance of rot in tomatoes anywhere except on the few plants bordering the asparagus bed where chip manure is used.

Senator Selkreg. Not the slightest. That is a matter that I observed particularly before any remarks were made about it. I saw fruit rotted in that place, and searched carefully to see how far the trouble prevailed. But there was no rot whatever anywhere except in that one place, where I was informed chip manure had been used, and rot was traceable to that cause."

We are convinced that well rotted barnyard manure, muck, where obtainable, or ordinary loam, or soil of bottom lands; soils of the prairies of the West, of the swamps and morasses of the East and the South, when mixed with forest leaves and composted with lime, salt and ashes in equal proportions, will prove, as top dressing, worth vastly more than the best of phosphates; and that what has been denominated green manuring, the plowing in of clover, buckwheat, rye-grass, etc. is of far greater value than the expensive fertilizers of which ordinary use is made.

We think it of value to our readers to give in this, the concluding chapter of our book, the following account of the proceedings at a late meeting of The American Pomological Society. The subjects discussed are of vital value to horticulturists and the information given upon them cannot be found elsewhere. The report was made for the *Press* of Philadelphia, by that able journalist, Mr. Chas. A. Green, Editor of *The Fruit Grower*, published in Rochester, N. Y., and we deem the subject matter of it as correlative with our new agriculture.

"The success of the twentieth annual meeting of the American Pomological Society recently held at Grand Rapids, Mich. was largely owing to the efforts of President Marshall P. Wilder, one of the best men ever engaged in the work; to acting President Patrick Barry, Prof. W. J. Beal, Charles W. Garfield, E. H. Scott and other prominent Michigan men.

"President Wilder in his address glanced at the thirty-seven years in which the society had worked. Long may it live on prospering, and to prosper while the earth bears fruit and man lives to cultivate it. This society is performing an immense amount of labor in correcting errors. There is a wonderful contrast between the early condition of pomology and that of the present day. The future work will be continuous, and of vital importance. Press on the good work, and when you are gone others will rise to take your places.

"Mr. Angel reported that Michigan produces five million bushels of large fruits annually, and that the prospects for the future are more promising. In the discussion of new fruits, the yellow transparent apple was spoken of by Mr. Gideon as about as hardy as the Oldenburg, which had suffered the past year, when the thermometer fell to forty-nine degrees below zero. The apple is of good quality and twelve days earlier than the Red Astrachan. It bears young and is of uniform size. It has a tendency to crack when over-ripe. It originated near St. Petersburg, Russia. The Shannon apple, which took the first premium at the World's Exposition at New Orleans, is a seedling from Arkansas. It is profitable in the North and West, is a large, showy fruit, but not of first quality. Mr. Gidcon considers the Oldenburg as hardy as any except the crabs. He had found nothing but the crabs that would endure the past winter, which was the most severe of any that they had experienced.

"Professor Bessey of Nebraska gave an illustrated lecture on Injurious Fungi. While most people look out upon the fields of grass, vegetables and fruits, considering that these cover the extent of plant life, Professor Bessey tells us that there is another race of plants often too small to be discovered by the naked eye, one differing from another, and each having as remarkable peculiarities, as the plants that are visible in our fields. This great race of plants, called Fungi, should be better understood by practical men and women, as it has much to do with the health of plants, trees and human beings. Forest trees four hundred feet in height differ from the particles of moss that thrive upon their trunks no more than one species of fungi differs from another in size. We often hear the remark made that certain disorders are caused by fungus growth. This would be something like stating that apples belong to the vegetable kingdom. It would scarcely mean anything, for there are as many kinds of fungus growth as of other plants, and each one has its peculiarities. The puff ball is referred to as one of the largest fungi. Fungi is divided into three classes —parasite, saprophytes and parasite-saprophytes. The parasites feed only upon living tissues, and the saprophytes feed only on dead matter, while the parasite-saprophytes are more greedy, and feed upon both living and dead matter, attacking more largely languishing tissues.

"William Saunders remarked that scientific men were for a long time puzzled to know whether bacteria belonged to the animal or vegetable kingdom. Professor Bessey treated them as plants. If an apple was magnified as we magnify bacteria under our best glasses, it would appear to be two and one-half miles in diameter.

The body of a man cut up into pieces, each of which was as small as a bacteria, and each piece placed before the other, would create a line of atoms of flesh one hundred and ninety million miles long, or long enough to pass around the earth six and one-half thousand times. This illustration will enable the reader to get an idea of the minuteness of these small plants, which may be floating in the air we breathe by the millions and yet not be observed. Bacteria reproduce themselves with wonderful rapidity. They withdraw a portion of the constituents of the vital part they attack, and thereby cause an enfeebled condition and ultimate destruction. There are many kinds of bacteria, each of which appears to have an important work in the economy of nature. It is wonderful to think that the Almighty brings about remarkable results from such infinitisimal creations. When the bodies of animals, plants and fruits have ceased to be of further use, it is desirable that they should be transformed into a condition where they may be absorbed and used in the construction of other forms. Bacteria seem to have been created largely for this work. Thus they assist to transform fallen logs into vegetable mould, and defunct animals and fruit into food supplies for other organisms. No doors or windows are close enough to keep out bacteria. Wherever the air can enter they can enter also.

"Professor Arthur, of the New Jersey Experimental Station, spoke of his experiments with pear blight. While Professor Burrill has previously claimed that pear blight was caused by bacteria, some of our most practical men throughout the country, like President Barry, of Rochester, N. Y., and others, have had serious doubts whether blight might not be the result rather than the cause. Professor Arthur's experiments have cleared up all doubts on this question. We know now the true cause of pear blight, and are in a much better condition to fight it than ever before. It is difficult to carry on warfare with an enemy that you know nothing of, and of whose identity you are uncertain, but once have him cornered as we now have the enemy of the pear, we shall no longer fear him. Our space will not permit giving a full description of Professor Arthur's thorough investigation. Suffice it to say that it was thoroughly convincing. He has found that bacteria can be conveyed to the pear only when the young wood is exceedingly soft, and never through old wood, or that which has become hardened, except it be through the young and immature twigs. Thus the bacteria may be conveyed to the older wood only through the bacteria that enters the tender wood. The bacteria enters the trees in July, and hardly ever in August or later. The bark of the branch attacked may be destroyed several weeks before the leaves turn black, as the leaves are sustained by the wood of the branch. Usually the leaves turn black suddenly during a hot day. This is the first notice the orchardist has of disease, but really the damage has been done weeks before. Bacteria do not enter the branches by contact of diseased branches with healthy ones, neither are they conveyed by the pruning knife. The bacteria gain entrance to the trees through the young and tender wood, through the blossoms, or through the fruits in rains, or conveyed by the winds, Also possibly by evaporation of moisture from the soil in which they have been multiplied. Bacteria progress through the limbs more rapidly in the warmest weather. They are not killed by the cold, but are unable to make such fast progress during winter. Those in the affected branches work slowly all winter, but perish about the time the trees leave out in the spring. Germs for inoculating bacteria were secured by cutting pieces of blighted wood and placing them in water, or fluid produced by boiling corn meal in water, or hay tea. Soon the liquid was filled with the germs. A few of these inserted in the tender wood caused disease in a short time. The germs in a diseased tree escape to the surface in a sticky substance ; they are washed free of the gum by the rain, dropping to the ground, multiply in decaying substances beneath the trees, or in wet places near by. Here they pass the winter, and may live for several years. They are borne in the air when dry by the wind, being so extremely minute that they may be thus borne and carried great distances, coming in contact with the tender twigs, or the centre of flowers, and finally into the tree, producing disease. Professor Arthur found that although he experimented with many kinds of bacteria germs, only those found in blighted pear trees caused blight.

"Professor Lazenby reports experiments showing that soil mulched with straw is invariably lower in temperature than ground unmulched, teaching that it was not desirable to mulch strawberries where late spring frosts were prevalent, as strawberries mulched would be injured more by the frost than those unmulched. The only method by which mulching would be valuable in preventing damage by late spring frosts is by keeping the mulch above the plants and not permit the blossoms to be exposed until the danger of frost is past.

"Mr. Pierce of Ohio said that there were thousands who did not know the delights of growing the finest flowers and fruits. Enlist your wife and children in your work, says Charles W. Garfield.

"Mr. Lyon considered that brevity is always desirable for names of new fruits. The name of the originator or introducer would rarely be found inappropriate, or the name of the place where the variety originated, and either will generally possess the advantage of requiring but a single word. While the wish to add a characteristic word, designed to convey an impression of superiority, causes the name to be cumbersome, it does not aid in distinguishing the variety.

"Professor Lazenby gave the result of experiments with the effects of pollen on the strawberry. He showed that in some seasons pistillate strawberries are influenced by the pollen of the varieties applied. A. J. Fuller concurred in this opinion, and the question was nearly decided to the satisfaction of all present, that it was possible to affect the flavor, size and form of the strawberry by the application of pollen to the pistillate varieties. Yet it was not claimed that the effect would be noticeable to the casual observer in all cases, or might not be of sufficient importance to be adopted by the market grower. Mr. Lazenby found that the Crescent strawberry, growing alone under a glass, would produce no berries when not fertilized.

"Professor A. J. Cook, of Michigan, delivered an illustrated lecture on Economic Etomology. It is known that the damage done by insects last year was two millions of dollars, and the unknown damage was probably as much more. The number of species of destructive insects is increasing every year, and the waring against them has become more important. Many of these insects are formidable for the reason that they have no bird foes in this country. An insect changes its taste and habits, often leaving one plant and attacking another. A few years ago California was free from injurious insects, but now it is thoroughly infested. Insects have foes that often suppress their depredations. A knowledge of these foes is absolutely necessary to the farmer and fruit grower, also a knowledge of the habits and life of insects. Imported insects are far more injurious than our native ones. They seem to take a new lease of life in this country, and are more ferocious and persistent in their efforts.

"One half pound of London purple to a barrel of water, or a spoonful of Paris green to a barrel of water, is recommended for spraying trees at the time when the blossoms are about to fall, to destroy the canker worm, codling moth and numerous other insects that are liable to do injury. This application could be made at an expense of from three to five cents per tree, and should be applied whether there is canker worm in the orchard or not. The canker worm is becoming far more prevalent each year throughout the country. As the codling moth should be treated to the poison even in the absence of the canker worm, it will be seen that there is no excuse for permitting the canker worm to defoliate the trees."

As we referred in a former chapter to the statement of Professor Roberts to us that clover roots had been traced to a depth of eighteen feet, the following communication sent by him to Mr. Chas. A. Green, Editor of that admirable monthly, *The Fruit Grower*, will be of interest ;

AGRICULTURAL DEPARTMENT, CORNELL UNIVERSITY.

ITHACA, N. Y., July 30, 1885.

Mr. Charles A. Green:

DEAR SIR :—The *Tribune* of July 14, containing an article on "The New Agriculture" is received. In it you say that Mr. Cole says that "Professor Roberts of Ithaca has told him that he has traced red clover roots to a depth of eighteen feet that were growing in a bed of gravel overlaying water." Mr. Cole must have misunderstood me, as it was corn roots not clover roots that I was speaking of to him when I visited his place the week before you were there. I have a clover root preserved in our museum two feet nine inches long, which was taken from the borders of a nearby cellar. The roots of this plant, which was one year old, were nearly traced to the depth of the cellar—four feet—but they were so delicate that it was impossible to preserve their entire length.

At the Iowa Agricultural College the railroad company undermined a portion of the corn field in August, 1873, to get gravel with which to ballast their road. Here I took great delight in studying corn roots. They were large enough to preserve at a depth of eight, but where the ground began to be moist from the water beneath, by careful digging they could be traced from two to four feet farther, where they reached perennial water.

As to the "New Agriculture" with pick and shovel, I most carefully examined the land treated by Mr. Cole, and also that adjoining which was not treated, and I expect in the near future to give some facts and my conclusions to the public.

Very respectfully yours,
I. P. ROBERTS.

We are growing old and anxious lest we die and see not in the flesh the fruits of our life-work—a half century spent in pursuit of the waters.

We want to see the tile manufacturers so conforming their wares as to conserve instead of wasting the waters.

We want to see the inventor at work giving the farmer a trenching machine which will do more subsoiling in a day than an hundred of the best plowmen can do now in a month with the most efficient implements, and doing it in a way which, once done, will not need to be done again.

We want to see an end of unfermented and uncomposted manures, and an end also of most of the phosphates with which the earth has been hitherto cursed.

We want to see farmers do their own fertilizing, avoiding seeds of fungus and fouling of lands by sowing inoculations of noxous plants and weeds.

In this latter connection it has occurred to us that the transportation from West to East of alkaline deposits, might be found profitable to both sections. The transit is made easy by means of our railroad system, so gridironing the country as to make interchange and admixture of soils less expensive than the use of phosphates The wonderful salt discoveries of the Wyoming Valley, making the use of brine and refuse salt for manure so inexpensive as to place them within reach of every farmer and gardener, is second only in importance to the discovery and development of petroleum and natural gas. These latter are already transported long distances through pipes, and we see no reason why alkaline and saline liquids may not be equally diffused by gravitation and made to reach all portions of our country.

In conclusion permit us to repeat our belief that an universal system of trenching will be adopted at an early day. We have proven that it is practical and profitable. We believe also that beyond in value of all present methods of fertilization, is that feature of "The New Agriculture" which extracts the solids from the waters furnishing food and inspiration to plant growth and fruition.

After reading these pages, indulgent reader, you fail to be convinced of the incalculable value of our system, or do not fully comprehend its details, we cordially invite you to come and see for yourself. The latchstring of our "Home on the Hillside" is hung on the outside of the door. A. N. COLE.

WELLSVILLE, ALLEGANY CO., N. Y.

The New Agriculture.

BUSINESS ANNOUNCEMENT.

A General Agent having been appointed for the United States of America, in the person of Theodore L. Minier, of Elmira, N. Y., all parties desiring information touching matters relating to business in connection with The New Agriculture, will address their communications to the General Agent.

State, Territorial, County and District Agencies will from time to time be created, and liberal commissions allowed to agents. Applications for agencies will be made to the General Agent, at Elmira, N. Y.

A Journal of Aquaculture.

ON WEDNESDAY, JANUARY, 6th, 1886,

A weekly journal will be issued under the title of

THE GENESEE VALLEY FREE PRESS AND NEW AGRICULTURE,

from the office of the "Daily Free Press," at Wellsville, Allegany Co., N. Y.

The Editorial Department of the paper will be patriotic rather than partisan. In upholding the Union and the Constitution it will know no North, no South, no East, no West.

Fully one-half of the paper will be devoted to Agriculture and Horticulture generally, and "The New Agriculture" in particular. I propose to edit the paper, and hold myself obligated to answer all questions that my correspondents may ask.

The paper will be a handsome quarto, and issued to subscribers at $2.00 per annum in advance.

A. N. COLE,

Wellsville, Allegany County, N. Y.

The American Angler.

THE FISHERMAN'S PAPER—THE ONLY ONE IN AMERICA.

THE AMERICAN ANGLER is published every Saturday, and each number contains essays on Fish, Fishing and Fish Culture, Notes and Queries relative to fishing and fish life, and practical illustrations of the methods and tackle used in angling. Drawings of seventy-five representative fish of America have already appeared in THE ANGLER, which is the only paper published in America devoted solely to Fish, Fishing and Fish Culture. Mr. Seth Green, the veteran Fish Culturist of America, has editorial charge of the Fish Culture Department of the paper.

Subscription per annum...$3 00
Single copies... 10

Back numbers of the paper can be had on application at 10 cents each, except those issued between the dates of October 15, 1881, and June 30, 1882, for which a charge of 25 cents each will be made. Specimen copies will be sent on application.

Address

THE AMERICAN ANGLER,
Offices: 252 Broadway, New York.

THE FISHES OF THE EAST ATLANTIC COAST,

THAT ARE

CAUGHT WITH HOOK AND LINE,

INCLUDING THE

FISHES of the EAST COAST of FLORIDA.

By Louis O. Van Doren and Samuel C. Clarke.

This is a practical text book on the salt water fishes that are found on the Atlantic coast from Northern Maine to the Gulf of Mexico. No other work now in print covers this field, and none has been published on this subject for the last quarter of a century. Messrs. Van Doren and Clarke give the scientific and popular descriptions, habits, habitat, WHEN, WHERE and HOW to catch them, of forty-two fishes that are caught with hook and line along the eastern coast of America. The illustrations are numerous and are photo-likenesses of the fish represented. They consist of the following:

THE STRIPED BASS.	THE BLACKFISH.
THE BLUEFISH.	THE FLOUNDER.
THE WEAKFISH.	THE SEA BASS.
THE SHEEPSHEAD.	THE BERGALL.
THE KINGFISH.	THE TOMCOD.
THE BONITO.	THE CODFISH.
THE BLACK DRUM.	THE HADDOCK.
THE SPANISH MACKEREL.	THE SALT WATER TROUT.
THE MENHADEN.	THE RED GROUPER.
THE LAFAYETTE, OR SPOT.	THE POMPANO.
THE SHAD.	THE MANGROVE SNAPPER.
THE TARPUM.	THE LADY FISH.
THE CHANNEL BASS.	THE SALT WATER CAT FISH.
THE HOGFISH.	THE WHITE, OR SILVER MULLET.

CLOTH, 16MO. PRICE, POST-PAID, $1.50

Address

THE AMERICAN ANGLER,

252 Broadway, New York.

PORTRAITS of FISHES.

At the request of many of our readers, we have struck off on fine gray tinted Bristol board, 7x11 inches each, a few copies of the following named fishes. They are sixty in number; twenty-three are engravings of those killed in fresh water, and thirty-seven in salt water. These fish portraits have been printed with much care, and will be of interest and service to those who wish to preserve them either framed or in a portfolio. We will mail them, postage paid, at the following prices.

The Fresh Water Series, (23 in number), for $2.00.
The Salt Water Series, (37 in number), for $3.50.
The entire series, (60 in number), for $5.00.
Single copies, ten cents.

THE FRESH WATER SERIES.

The Small-Mouthed Black Bass.
The Large-Mouthed Black Bass.
The Brook Trout.
The Grayling.
The California Mountain Trout.
The California Salmon.
The Pike Perch.
The Land-Locked Salmon.
The Sea Salmon.
The Pike.
The Lake Lawyer.
The Salmon Trout.
The Mascalonge.
The Yellow Perch.
The Whitefish.
The Fresh Water Striped Bass.
The White Perch.
The Bisby Trout.
The Shad.
The Lake Herring.
The Bream.
The Strawberry Bass.
The Rock Bass.

THE SALT WATER SERIES.

The Striped Bass.
The Blue Fish.
The Sheepshead.
The Channel Bass.
The Pompano.
The Red Grouper.
The Lady Fish.
The Spanish Mackerel.
The Salt Water Trout, Florida.
The Weakfish.
The Bonito.
The Kingfish.
The Sea Bass.
The Red Snapper.
The Blackfish.
The Porgy.
The Pilot Fish.
The Lafayette, or Spot.
The Hogfish.
The Menhaden.
The Codfish.
The Tarpum.
The Mangrove Snapper.
The Haddock.
The Butterfish.
The Smelt.
The Black Drum.
The Squid.
The Codling.
The Unicorn Fish.
The Moon Fish.
The Spotted Turbot.
The Northern Sculpin.
The Bergall.
The Flounder.
The Salt Water Catfish, Gafftopsail.
The White Mullet.

A handsome Portfolio, in half Russia, with bevelled edges, and stamped in gilt "Fish Portraits," made especially to hold a set of fishes, will be mailed, postage paid, on receipt of $1.25.

Address, AMERICAN ANGLER,
252 Broadway, New York.

THE ANGLER'S SCORE BOOK

AND

Fishing Register.

On the opposite page is given a full page illustration (exact size) of this handy score book. It contains a sufficient number of pages for a season's record, and will be found indispensable to the angler who feels sufficient interest in his pastime to derive pleasure and profit from his past achievements.

It is bound in heavy paper, price 10 cents, and in limp cloth and gold, 25 cents. Pocket size.

AMERICAN ANGLER,
252 Broadway, New York.

FISH SCORE.

If you wish your Score published, fill up this blank, sign your name and mail it to the "AMERICAN ANGLER", New York.

Date............188... Town ....

County................ State ....

Name of Water ....

SPECIES OF FISH CAUGHT.	Number	Weight of Largest	Total Weight	Size of Largest	Baits used
....					
....					
....					
....					

State of Water..................
State of Weather..................
Wind..................

FISH SCORE

Date........................
Town........................
County........................
State........................
Name of Water........................

FISH CAUGHT.

....
....
....
....

Baits used..................
Weight of Largest..................
Size of Largest..................
State of Water..................
State of Weather..................
Direction of Wind..................

TEXT PAPERS FOR ANGLERS.

The six volumes, handsomely bound in cloth (after July 1, 1885, seven vol.), of THE AMERICAN ANGLER, are now ready for delivery. Price $3.00 each. The demand for the unbound numbers of Volume I. has so largely decreased our supply of them, that we are compelled to increase the price of copies to 25 cents each. New subscribers, however, who commence their subscriptions with the first issue of the paper, October 1, 1881, will be supplied at the regular rate of $3.00 a year.

To assist our readers, who are daily ordering back numbers, in the selection of those containing special treatises of practical value to anglers, we give below a few of the dates and a partial list of subjects contained in Volumes II, III and IV. They will be sent, postage paid, on receipt of ten cents for each copy.

What is a Pike? What is a Pickerel? Illustrated. December 16, 1882.
A Sole Leather Bait Box. Illustrated, December 23, '82.
Striking and Playing a Fish. December 30, '82.
The White Perch. Illustrated. December 30, '82.
A Treatise on the Mascalonge—Where, When and How to Catch Them. Illustrated. Contained in the issues of January 6, 13, 20, 27, '83.
A Treatise on the Black Bass—Habitat, Modes of Capture, etc. Illustrated. In issues of February 3, 10, 17, 24, '83.
The Strawberry Bass. Illustrated. February 17, '83.
A Treatise on the Pike—Habitat, tackle used, etc. Illustrated. In issues of March 3, 10, 17, 24, '83.
The Reel—Its place on the Rod. March 24, April 14, June 16, '83.
The Atlantic Salmon. Scientific and Popular Description—Habitat and capture. Illustrated. March 31, '83.
Minnows as Bait. Illustrated April 7, 14, 21, '83.
Catching Flounders. Illustrated. April 7, '83.
The Trout of Maine Waters. April 14, 21, 28, May 5, '83.
The Trout Streams of the United States and How to Reach Them. April 14, '83.
A Serviceable Fishing Boat—How to Build it. Illustrated. April 21, '83.
Making a Split Bamboo—Amateur Work. April 28, '83.
Varnish for Rods. May 5, 83.
A Treatise on the Brook Trout—Habits, Habitat and Capture. Illustrated May 12, 19, 26, June 2, '83.
The Colorado Mountain Trout. May 12, '83.
A New Minnow Pail. Illustrated. May 12, 1883.
The Striped Bass—Rock Fish—Description, Modes of Capture, etc. Illustrated. May 26, June 2, '83.

Any of the above papers sent postpaid on receipt of ten cents.

Address   THE AMERICAN ANGLER,
252 Broadway, New York.

www.ingramcontent.com/pod-product-compliance
Lightning Source LLC
Chambersburg PA
CBHW020808230426
43666CB00007B/906